Praise for
Enneagram Made Easy

"Learning the Enneagram is much more than reading about nine types. It is most centrally a journey into the heart of compassion—for oneself and for our fellow human beings. And you will find no finer guide on this journey than Dr. Deborah Egerton. *Enneagram Made Easy* is an excellent entry into this work. Highly Recommended."

Russ Hudson, Cofounder of the Enneagram Institute, Author of *The Enneagram: Nine Gateways to Presence*, and Co-author of *The Wisdom of the Enneagram*

"In *Enneagram Made Easy*, Dr. Deborah Egerton elegantly unravels the intricate depths of the soul through the Enneagram, rendering the complex into the accessible. This journey of self-discovery breathes life into abstract concepts, grounding them in our reality. Dr. Egerton's wisdom gently guides readers to the revelation that the treasure they seek is, in fact, the gold within themselves."

Catherine Bell, CEO and Author of *The Awakened Company*

"Deborah Egerton is one of the world's leading practitioners of the Enneagram, but more importantly she brings this information with such deep compassion and a fierce love for all of humanity. This is a wonderful book to explore this amazing system of Unity."

Colette Baron-Reid, Spiritual Medium, Acclaimed Oracle Expert, and Best-selling Author of *The Map*

"In a short space of time, Deborah Egerton, who I lovingly call 'Dr. E.' has not only helped me understand the Enneagram, but also supported me in applying its healing principles to my life and relationships. I had been thinking to myself 'I wish everyone could have a Dr. E'—and now with *Enneagram Made Easy*, you can!"

KYLE GRAY, BEST-SELLING AUTHOR OF *RAISE YOUR VIBRATION* AND *ANGEL PRAYERS*

"This book will change the relationship you have with yourself and everyone else. I love Dr. E.; her work is so helpful, important, inspiring, and inspired."

REBECCA CAMPBELL, BEST-SELLING AUTHOR OF *RISE SISTER RISE* AND *LETTERS TO A STARSEED*

"*Enneagram Made Easy* is one of the most helpful books for KNOWING YOURSELF AND OTHERS that I've read. And it's written by one of the wisest and most loving Enneagram teachers on the planet!"

ROBERT HOLDEN, BEST-SELLING AUTHOR OF *SHIFT HAPPENS!* AND *HAPPINESS NOW!*

"Dive into the transformative world of the Enneagram with a book that's as enlightening as it is heartwarming. If you're ready to embark on a journey of self-discovery and understanding others like never before, this book is your guiding light."

GABRIELLE BERNSTEIN, #1 *NEW YORK TIMES* BEST-SELLING AUTHOR OF *THE UNIVERSE HAS YOUR BACK*

ENNEAGRAM
Made Easy

Also in the *Made Easy* series

ENNEAGRAM
Made Easy

Explore the Nine Personality Types
of the Enneagram to Open Your Heart,
Find Joy, and Discover Your True Self

DEBORAH THREADGILL EGERTON, Ph.D.
with Lisi Mohandessi

HAY HOUSE
Carlsbad, California • New York City
London • Sydney • New Delhi

Published in the United Kingdom by:
Hay House UK Ltd, The Sixth Floor, Watson House,
54 Baker Street, London W1U 7BU
Tel: +44 (0)20 3927 7290; www.hayhouse.co.uk

Published in the United States of America by:
Hay House Inc., PO Box 5100, Carlsbad, CA 92018-5100
Tel: (1) 760 431 7695 or (800) 654 5126
www.hayhouse.com

Published in Australia by:
Hay House Australia Pty Ltd, 18/36 Ralph St, Alexandria NSW 2015
Tel: (61) 2 9669 4299; www.hayhouse.com.au

Published in India by:
Hay House Publishers India, Muskaan Complex,
Plot No.3, B-2, Vasant Kunj, New Delhi 110 070
Tel: (91) 11 4176 1620; www.hayhouse.co.in

Text © Deborah Threadgill Egerton, 2024

The information given in this book should not be treated as a substitute
for professional medical advice; always consult a medical practitioner.
Any use of information in this book is at the reader's discretion and
risk. Neither the author nor the publisher can be held responsible for
any loss, claim or damage arising out of the use, or misuse, of the
suggestions made, the failure to take medical advice or for any material
on third-party websites.

A catalogue record for this book is available from the British Library.

Tradepaper ISBN: 978-1-4019-7589-0
E-book ISBN: 978-1-4019-7590-6
Audiobook ISBN: 978-1-4019-7591-3

Interior illustrations © Lisi Mohandessi

10 9 8 7 6 5 4 3 2 1

Printed in the United States of America

This product uses papers sourced from responsibly managed forests.
For more information, see www.hayhouse.com.

'Make everything as simple as possible, but not simpler.'

ALBERT EINSTEIN

Contents

PART II: THE POINTS

PART III: FINDING YOUR PLACE ON THE ENNEAGRAM MAP

Introduction

The Enneagram, with its intricate layers and profound insights, is a testament to the wisdom from Albert Einstein that opens this book. It is not an endeavor to be approached with haste or to be condensed into quick fixes and cheat sheets. Rather, it requires patience, curiosity, and a commitment to delve into its depths at a reasonable pace.

In *Enneagram Made Easy*, we intentionally crafted a guide that introduces you to the fundamental concepts and shared language of the Enneagram, ensuring that you have a solid foundation before diving into the vast pool of wisdom that this system offers. It is my hope that more people will take the time to understand these fundamentals, allowing them to approach their journey with clarity and a strong sense of self-awareness.

You may choose to skim the surface, seeking a glimpse of what the Enneagram has to offer. And within the pages of this book, you will find a wealth of knowledge and information. However, should you decide to embrace the fullness of the Enneagram, I assure you that the guidance within these pages will be a steadfast companion on your lifelong journey of self-discovery.

Studying the Enneagram is not a destination; it is an ongoing exploration that brings you ever closer to the essence of your being. It is our sincere hope that *Enneagram Made Easy* will serve as a trusted companion, providing you with the necessary tools to embark on this transformative journey.

I extend this invitation to you with open arms, knowing that your unique perspective and experiences will contribute to the rich tapestry of the Enneagram community. Your support and engagement will not only enhance your personal growth but also inspire others to embrace the transformative power of the Enneagram.

Together, let us embark on a journey of self-discovery, empowering ourselves and others to live lives of authenticity and fulfillment.

Try to resist the urge to "just read about yourself." The Enneagram is a fluid system that provides access to all nine types. I refer to them as points to encourage you, the reader, to explore your relationship with every single one of these energies. If you only look at the one point that happens to be yours, you will be depriving yourself of a rich experience. I would compare that to receiving nine beautifully wrapped presents, each containing a different gift for you, but you only choose to open one.

Finding your place on the Enneagram map is an essential first step. You lead from this point. It is your home base, your default that you return to, and the dominant energy that you embody. The ancient Greek aphorism "Know thyself" is "applied to those whose boasts exceed what they are" and is also a warning to pay no attention to the opinion of the multitude. These words are said to be inscribed on the walls of the Temple of Apollo at Delphi. These words have great significance in our ever-evolving and rapidly changing world. When you picked up this book, you began your journey to discover who you really are instead of creating another version of yourself. It is quite the opposite of You 2.0. Your goal now is to find out who you are underneath all the versions of yourself that you have created. Welcome to the journey of your lifetime! May you find joy, peace, acceptance, and belonging in this exploration. May love be your path and light shine on every step you take. Most importantly, may you fall deeply in love with the authentic you. The glorious being that you were created to be.

Part I

GETTING STARTED

Chapter 1

History

The Enneagram is an archetypal personality system that combines modern psychological practices with a deep foundation in ancient traditions, religions, cultures, and spiritual practices. It is a model of the human psyche taught as a typology of nine points and personality types. These points have names that reflect the nine different energies: Challenger, Peacemaker, Idealist, Helper, Achiever, Individualist, Investigator, Loyalist, and Enthusiast.

Where Did It Come From?

The Enneagram has an extensive and multifaceted background. The nine-pointed symbol stemming from the Greek words *ennea* (nine) and *grammos* (a written model/point), has a fascinating history interwoven across various cultures and traditions and among mathematicians, philosophers, theologians, and psychologists throughout time. Some argue that the Enneagram was always there, it just needed to be uncovered, and that the modern Enneagram system emerged from a collective consciousness over many lifetimes.

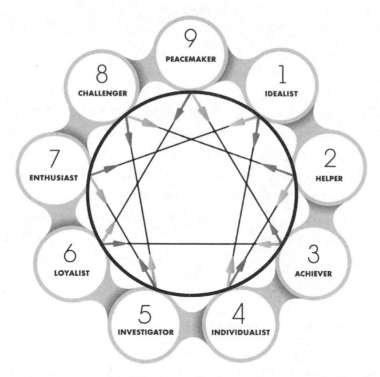

The Enneagram map

Many Enneagram scholars believe the symbol is traceable to the sacred geometry of Pythagorean mathematics. Additionally, in the ancient work of Plotinus, the founder of Neoplatonism and a student of Plato, he refers to nine divine qualities that manifest in human nature. His work expanded on human nature by defining the duality of every person as the physical body and the existence of the soul or cognitive agency. Later on we begin to see the roots of the modern Enneagram system appearing in different forms across multiple spiritual and theological traditions. Christianity, Judaism, branches of the Tree of Life in the Kabbalah, Islam, Jesuit mathematics, and Buddhism are all practices where we find the influence of the Enneagram. It was an incredible experience for me personally to see essential elements of the Enneagram in the hieroglyphics inscribed in the ruins of the ancient Egyptians.

George Gurdjieff, an Armenian philosopher and mystic, is often credited with reintroducing the symbol into the modern world in the 19th century with his application of it to different aspects of life. Gurdjieff did not teach the Enneagram as a personality-typing mechanism but rather as a way of seeing and becoming aware of the order of things. He proposed that the map of the nine points could illustrate and reflect how the human consciousness operates and functions in distinguishable patterns. He used the symbol to explain the unfolding of creation, calling it a symbol of perpetual motion. He claimed that unity and diversity could coexist in harmony—within the symbol we see the circle representing unity, the triangle representing the individual, and the hexad representing change and dynamism. The origin of Gurdjieff's education and the foundation of the Enneagram is slightly ambiguous. He claimed to have been introduced to the Enneagram in the 1920s during a stay at a monastery in Afghanistan.

We received a priceless gift from the book *In Search of the Miraculous Fragments of an Unknown Teaching* by P.D. Ouspensky. It is our best source for exploring Gurdjieff's work. In this book, Pyotr Ouspensky, a student of Gurdjieff, captured a detailed account of his teachings. Many years later, in the 1950s, Oscar Ichazo expanded upon Gurdjieff's work and began to connect modern psychology, the patterns of human behavior, and the functionality of the symbol—a collection of theories that he called *protoanalysis* (nine different ways of being in the world). During the 1970s, we experienced a wave of human enlightenment and began to see psychologists, philosophers, and psychiatrists revolutionize how we view human behavior and humanity in and of itself. During that time, Chilean psychiatrist Claudio Naranjo pioneered the modern Enneagram system as we know it today. He connected the ancient works of the world's great philosophers, Gurdjieff's exploration of the symbol, and Ichazo's recognition of measurable patterns within the human psyche. As he developed the system, he began to teach small groups and communities of people, who then took his work and expanded it even further. Many of his early teachings were done in small Christian communities and, most notably, a group he formed called the SAT, Seekers After Truth, in California.

From Naranjo, we can see the Enneagram's inner mechanisms unfold from different teachers and psychologists, including Levels of Development, Instincts, harmonics, and so on. The early pioneers of the modern system who studied under Claudio Naranjo include but are not limited to teachers such as Sandra Maitri, A.H. Almaas, Fr. Robert Ochs, Don Riso, Russ Hudson, and Beatrice Chestnut. Hameed Ali, who writes under the pseudonym A.H. Almaas, developed the spiritual path called the Diamond Approach to Inner Realization after participating in the first SAT group with Naranjo, Maitri, and Ochs. Sandra Maitri joined Almaas in the Diamond Approach practice, and they developed many Enneagram programs together. Fr. Ochs brought the Enneagram into the Catholic church. According to the Australian Institute for Enneagram Studies, "In the 1970s, Catholic theology students were taught the Enneagram in Chicago by Fr. Ochs. Ochs changed the Enneagram to suit his theological purpose of integrating the Enneagram with the teachings of St. Ignatius Loyola.

In doing so, Ochs radically changed the Enneagram and fundamentally altered its diagnostic purpose."

A few years after the initial SAT group in Berkeley was formed, Don Riso began his Enneagram path within the Jesuit community and developed his methods for Enneagram exploration. His work, which Carl Gustav Jung and Karen Horney also influenced, expanded the Enneagram into a deep level of inquiry. Shortly after he began his studies, Russ Hudson joined him. Together, they pioneered many of the more recent applications and influenced how practitioners use and incorporate the wisdom of the Enneagram to this day. In 1991 Riso and Hudson developed the RHETI (Riso-Hudson Enneagram Type Indicator), a scientifically validated questionnaire that has been used and respected as one of the leading Enneagram tests for over 30 years *(see page 246–47)*. In 1997 they founded the Enneagram Institute, a school that people traveled to from around the world for its awe-inspiring collection of Enneagram wisdom.

As the Enneagram is mysterious and complex by nature, so is the unfolding of its wisdom, as clearly illustrated in its background. Russ Hudson, the co-author of the highly renowned book *The Wisdom of the Enneagram*, argues that the Enneagram is not a personality system designed to pigeonhole or box a person in but rather a guide to provide opportunities to see a new trajectory for growth and awareness. He continues by saying that the Enneagram is a map of our essence and helps us uncover how we have fallen asleep to our true nature. In an interview, Hudson refers to the Enneagram as a "tool for discerning how we lose track of presence."

In that respect, consider viewing the Enneagram as a dynamic system full of possibility, not as a restrictive code of rules and regulations. It is fluid by nature and allows for the unfolding of mysteries and wonders life offers if we are willing to stay present enough to *witness* the unfolding.

What Does It Do?

The Enneagram invites you to explore your way of being. It opens the door to understanding many of the unique mechanisms behind how you function, such as why you do the things you do and how you operate daily to meet your needs. Understanding your basic motivation, values, fears, and the strengths that you have to offer are gifts that keep on giving. At the same time, some things are intrinsic to the egoic structures that trip us up, preventing us from being a person who can honor our authentic selves. More importantly, while the Enneagram can help us find ourselves, it will also help us find others through connection, appreciation, and presence.

When studied and implemented correctly, the Enneagram teaches us how to be together in a community through connection and interrelatedness. The concept of unity and diversity coexisting in harmony represented within the symbol comes alive.

The Enneagram helps us see the circle representing unity and live the reality of our universal oneness. In contrast, the triangle represents the individual and validates the soul's search for the authentic self of each individual. The hexad, meaning change and dynamism, helps us understand and live within the dynamic flow of an ever-changing and fluid reality. Our ability to relate to one another depends on how we invest our time and efforts into understanding the connections. The Enneagram provides us with a road map and guidance for this journey. As you explore your being, you will discover that the more you know about yourself, the better the quality of your relationships, including your core relationship with yourself.

This road map for your journey and blueprint
of your soul is the instruction manual that
we all wish we had been born with.

In my book *Know Justice Know Peace: A Transformative Journey of Social Justice, Anti-Racism, and Healing through the Power of the Enneagram*, I expand on this concept:

As individuals, we have a natural tendency to look toward the external to correct things that are not working well for our individual way of being. If I were to ask you, "Whose attitudes, behaviors, and beliefs can you control?" your response is likely to be, "Only my own." While we know the correct answer to this question, we do not live our lives in a way that is aligned with that response. We may know that this is true. However, our tendency is to expect other people to change their behavior to fit our personal wants and needs. Let it suffice to say that there are few among us who cannot come up with a list of ways that we would like the people around us to change their behaviors. Especially if those behaviors affect you personally.

We can elevate the level of consciousness around how we experience people during interactions and how their actions, behaviors, and beliefs affect us if we are willing to do our own work. The Enneagram can help us peel back the layers of our internal programming to release what no longer serves us for our growth and the greater good. Inner work involves waking up and becoming present to how you show up in the world. When you begin to notice how your attitudes, behaviors, and beliefs have you trapped in a fortress of judgmental binary thinking, you begin to do inner work. Inquiry without judgment and expansion of your heart space is the resulting awareness from this work. Learning about and understanding yourself in terms of what drives and motivates you is essential. Becoming more open and accepting that we do not all have the same way of moving through the world and how you relate with others based on what drives and motivates them is all part of doing your inner work. It is how we are able to move beyond dehumanizing people by no longer seeing them as objects or pawns in the game of life but rather moving toward honoring the humanity of every individual and thus regaining our own humanity. We can allow ourselves to experience the world around us in a new way. A kinder, more compassionate, and more loving community must emerge. This can only happen if we do our individual work and come together as a community that treats no one as less than another but rather seeks to elevate each individual to reach their highest and best. This is how we come to know peace.

As human beings, we have a deep-rooted drive or desire to belong. This drive is different for every human being and is relative based on the individual's environment, culture, dimensions of diversity, Enneagram point, and a multitude of other factors. However, the desire to belong and find our place is usually at the core of our actions, behaviors, and beliefs and affects how we navigate the world. As we are trying to establish where we fit in and how we can feel like we belong, we can become trapped in our personality structures and lose sight of our true purpose and sense of belonging. This is where the power of the Enneagram can illuminate our true path and any obstacles that may be in our way. Through the Enneagram, we can begin to:

❖ explore how our personality shapes our inner drive to belong

❖ unravel any self-betraying manipulations we may have constructed

❖ determine our actual place in the world based on embracing our authentic selves

❖ let go of what no longer serves us and continue our journey of self-discovery and reconnection

❖ make our unique contributions by reigniting our passion and standing in our purpose

Throughout this book, I will share an in-depth exploration of the different components that make up each point, including the basic desire, basic fear, core motivation, passion, fixation, virtue, Levels of Development, and the inner dynamics or connections within the points. These are the building blocks of the Enneagram and will serve as your foundational education as you begin your Enneagram journey.

I will also briefly explore the Instincts, sometimes called subtypes, within each Enneagram energy: Self-Preservation, Social, and Sexual. Exploring the Instincts requires deeply investigating how each point can manifest differently. Using the three different Instincts within each Enneagram energy produces 27 unique instinctual variants. I will introduce you briefly to the Instincts, and hopefully you will continue your Enneagram journey to discover all the components that make up your specific Enneagram energy. You will also receive a glimpse into real-life testimonials of people who stand at each of the nine points on the Enneagram map. For some people just beginning their exploration into the Enneagram, real-life examples can help illustrate how the energy shows up from a more personal perspective.

You will find a condensed overview of deeper elements of the Enneagram toward the end of the book. There are many more components to the Enneagram, and though we outline some of them here, I encourage you to open yourself to the vastness found in the unfolding. The Enneagram is complex and has many applications and approaches to utilizing its wisdom. If you want to continue your Enneagram journey beyond the basics provided in this book, you can refer to the resources on pages 257–58.

But first we need to learn to crawl before we walk, let alone run. So let's start at the beginning with the basics of the Enneagram.

Chapter 2

The Elements
of the Enneagram

Now that you know the history of the Enneagram and have a brief idea of how it works, it's time that we decode some of the terms that you'll hear when people are talking about the Enneagram.

Point/Type

Energy exists everywhere. Our words have a specific energy, as do our attitudes, behaviors, and beliefs. There are distinct energies at each of the nine points of the Enneagram. When we talk about an Enneagram point/type, we refer to the place on the Enneagram where you embody the most substantial energy, but remember we have access to all nine points. When you explore all nine points, you may feel a connection to many of them; however, the energy at one of the points will be your dominant energy or what is referred to in Enneagram teaching as your type. Sometimes the word type creates resistance and is experienced as being put in a box. I have had many clients and students who use their identification with a particular type as an excuse for bad behavior. "Don't be mad; you know I'm a Seven!" "I'm not moody; I'm a Four!" or "I'm not being critical; you know I am a One!" I have listened to that long enough that I have intentionally chosen to be mindful of my language when I teach the Enneagram.

There is something freeing about identification with point versus type, though it is essential to understand why both terms are helpful. As a person who stands at Enneagram Point One, I feel free to move around to the other points and experience the different energies. Just as we make choices about many things that do or do not work for us, you are free to think of yourself as a particular type or as standing at one specific point from which you lead or start. Do what works for you while you are finding your way on this journey. Those of us who write about or teach the Enneagram are here as your guides, and we cannot determine your type or point. That is part of your journey, and we are simply here to walk beside you as you explore a powerful way to do your inner work. Throughout this book, we will use the words point and type interchangeably.

Remember that we start at Point Eight and continue clockwise through the Enneagram map to address the points in each center as a group instead of going in numerical order. The order is as follows:

Eight—Nine—One—
Two—Three—Four—
Five—Six—Seven

Centers of Intelligence

The Enneagram is explored through three centers: Body, Heart, and Head. Sometimes these centers, or triads, are called Body/Instinctive, Heart/Feeling, and Head/ Thinking. Each center has a connection to particular emotions: The Body is connected to anger and rage, the Heart to shame and guilt, and the Head to fear and anxiety. Points Eight, Nine, and One reside within the Body Center. Points Two, Three, and Four reside within the Heart Center. And finally, Points Five, Six, and Seven reside within the Head Center. If you are still in the early stages of your Enneagram journey and are trying to determine your type or point, exploring the centers may help you find where you land on the Enneagram map. The energy of each of these centers is palpable. With time and intentional inner work, you can discern when your centers are not in alignment. It is important to remember that we are composed of all three centers and can access our Body, Heart, and Head Centers at any given moment.

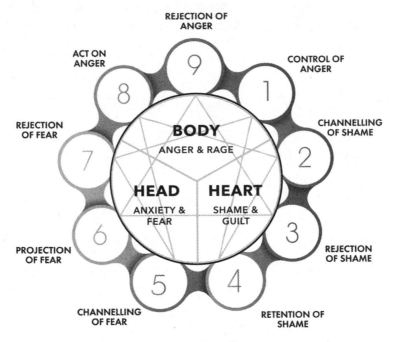

The Centers of Intelligence

Basic Fear

Each point has a basic fear: how we rationalize what we do and feel, and how we navigate obstacles throughout our lives. In some cases, the basic fear directly opposes our basic desire; for some people, it is how we avoid showing up authentically as our true selves. While we all have universal fears, there are specific fears that create patterns of behavior associated with each point. For example, the basic fear of a person standing at Point Seven can manifest as being trapped in relationships that feel suffocating or in painfully adverse circumstances. Being overwhelmed ultimately leads to restlessness and a strong, at times uncontrollable, urge to move toward something or someone more desirable. When repeated over time, this behavior pattern is the opposite of the desired effect. Later in the book, when we describe the basic fears for each point, note what comes up for you. If you strongly respond to a specific basic fear, it might be worth exploring regardless of where you fall on the Enneagram map.

Basic Desire

Many people who challenge this particular aspect of the Enneagram argue that "we all want to be happy" or "we all want to be loved." While this may be true, the desire to be loved or happy has conditions for each of us. For example, as a human who stands at Point One, my basic desire is to be good and to do the right thing. Being happy and being loved comes with the conditions of being good and doing the right thing. We will look at this more throughout the book, but the main takeaway is to avoid trying to box yourself in or get caught up in trying to resist exploring your personality at a deeper level. Determining your basic desire is critical in finding your dominant energy on the Enneagram map. Reflecting on your life as you have experienced it thus far, you can begin to look at some of the moments that you found to be memorable. Explore the emotions that you experienced and what was happening to you at a deeper level. You may be able to surface some new patterns, answers, or unhealed wounds to address.

Core Motivation

When the basic desire and the basic fear come together, assisted by the energy of the core wound in the background of our functionality, we experience the complexity of the core motivation. The core motivation constantly challenges us to get what we most desire at any given moment while avoiding what we fear will cause our demise. Unrevealed or dismissed core wounds also skew our behavioral patterns. The core motivation is your internal drive, the reason you wake up in the morning, how you navigate life, and that thing that gets you going or paralyzes you. Think of the core motivation as why you do what you do. It is the factor that drives most of your decisions, consciously or subconsciously, and it is how your personality navigates life. For example, at Point Four, there is a desire to be authentic and unique without falling into the ordinary or trendy. A melancholy comes from the core wound of feeling out of place or not belonging. The core motivation is often referred to as simply the basic desire; however, as it is usually compensation for the core fear, these two are the essential elements that drive your engine with your core wounds, adding additional fuel to the journey.

Wings

On either side of your dominant Enneagram point are two points referred to as wings. For instance, Point One has easy access to the energies of the Nine and Two wings. Point Two has access to One and Three, Three to Two and Four, and so on. Every Enneagram type has two wings; however, one of the wings may have a more significant influence on the energy of your dominant Enneagram type/point. This is one of the many reasons that two people who share the same dominant point can have subtle yet discernible differences in how they appear. As the Enneagram piques your interest, you will learn more about these concepts. It's important to remember that this is not a cookie-cutter system but rather a highly evolved complex schematic that respects the uniqueness of the individual and the influence of nature, nurture, parental overlay, and a multitude of other factors. The energy of your wings can also enable some points to access the other centers despite having no direct arrows.

As you begin to read and engage in the inner work, explore the points on either side of your dominant Enneagram point; you may find helpful information in your search for alignment of your three Centers of Intelligence.

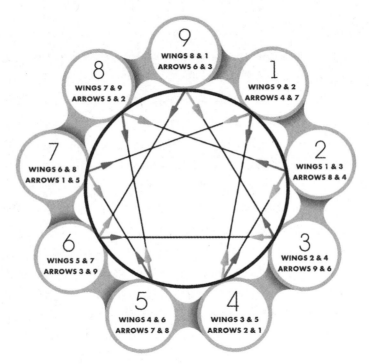

Wings, lines, and arrows

Lines and Arrows

The Enneagram lines and arrows, also referred to as the stress and security points or directions of growth and stress, connect the points across the map. Some

Enneagram practitioners use the arrows as one-way streets during stress and development, leaning into the perspective that you either go one way or the other. Up or down. Stress or growth. There is an expanded perspective on this as we gain recognition that the Enneagram offers us the gift of fluidity. We do not have to get stuck moving in one direction, believing that we only have access to the low side of our stress point or the high side of our growth point.

There are multiple ways of using the lines and arrows when we see them as connections to pick up specific qualities at specific times. For instance, some practitioners believe during times of conflict and stress, a Five will move to the unhealthy energy of Seven and become scattered, impulsive, hypercritical, and unable to see things through to completion. In the same context, during moments of growth and security, a Five will move to the healthy energy of Eight, becoming grounded, confident, more decisive, and communicative. These are the "one-way streets."

In contrast, we can have more fluidity in movement with the arrows. By embracing the fluidity of the arrows, the Five can move back and forth between the healthy and unhealthy energies of Point Seven and Eight as they experience stress and growth. It is essential to use the arrows as access to the gifts of each point or even use the unhealthy energy as a warning system to correct our actions and behaviors. We can move freely between these connections, picking up positive and negative energies. It's essential to accept that there are positive and negative qualities to acknowledge during stress. These qualities can catalyze growth and help us find our authentic selves. The energy we pick up from our arrows or lines can also facilitate the movement to other points when needed—especially for the points that face the chasm between centers.

Passion: The Way We Suffer

Each point holds a specific passion, sometimes aligned with the deadly sins concept. The book *The Wisdom of the Enneagram* describes passion as "the root of our imbalance and the way we become trapped in ego." The passions represent the nine main ways we lose our center, become more susceptible to personality distortions, and become disoriented from reality. It is an essential part of who we are, yet we try to reject rather than respect the power of this part of our being. The rejection or lack of acknowledgment of our passions can leave us paralyzed in a toxic pattern of behavior that distorts our true selves. For example, at Point Nine, the passion is called sloth. This moniker can be confusing because sloth as a descriptor here does not align accurately with the definition. In the case of the Nine, a more accurate description is self-forgetting. We will also explore the passions as the personal challenge we often cannot see or accept within ourselves. While our passion is ever-present, it does not need to negatively control our actions, behaviors, and beliefs. Instead, we invite you to examine your passion and use it in your shadow work as a warning system to recognize when your actions, behaviors, and beliefs set you up to become trapped in your fixation.

Fixation: How We Get Stuck

We all have a way of becoming trapped in our personality, which we see play out through the fixation. These "traps" are mental blocks we hold on to when attempting to justify our reality. Once again, the shadow self and egoic agenda have control of the wheel. For example, at Point Eight, the fixation described as vengeance justifies the subsequent actions taken, distorted beliefs held, and a felt sense of emotions. The fixation of personality is a distortion of our true selves and a tricky obstacle to overcome.

Virtue: The Gift of Our True Nature

Honoring the essence of our true selves and nurturing our growth requires us to embrace our virtues. It is through embodying these virtues that we truly come into alignment with our authentic selves and cultivate the qualities that allow us to thrive. These specific characteristics manifest through the emotional awareness of the authentic self, letting go of ego, self-deception, and dynamic vices. When we access our virtue, we become selfless and altruistic in our actions, feelings, and beliefs. An example of this transformative process at Point Six occurs when we see doubt and fear left behind and witness courage emerge as the virtue. A deep dive into the inner work is crucial in accessing the virtue at each point.

The passion can be used as a wake-up call to remove yourself from the trap of your fixation. By acknowledging both the passion and fixation, we are able to uncover the path to our virtue where we can reconnect to our authentic self and begin the healing process.

Instincts/Subtypes

The Instincts, sometimes referred to as subtypes and instinctual variants, within each Enneagram energy are Self-Preservation, Social, and Sexual (sometimes referred to as One-on-One).

The Instincts can be mirrored in the three drives for survival:

❖ preserving life and focusing on physical needs

❖ mutual cooperation and creating social bonds

❖ survival of the species through exploration and experiencing energies

The Self-Preservation instinct manifests as protecting and preserving the body and functions for basic survival. The Social instinct focuses on maintaining connections with others and creating social bonds. The Sexual instinct, or One-on-One, is the drive to extend ourselves into our environment and our attraction or chemistry with other people.

As balanced human beings, we have all three Instincts within us; however, we have a dominant instinct that we feel most comfortable with and a secondary instinct to support the dominant one. The third instinct is the least developed, therefore an area that manifests as an unseen personal challenge.

Gaining a comprehensive understanding of the Instincts necessitates a thorough exploration of the nuanced ways in which each Enneagram point can manifest differently. The distinctive characteristics of each Instinct within each point shed light on how the energies can manifest in diverse ways depending on which Instinct takes precedence in our daily lives. By considering the three different Instincts within the Enneagram, we uncover a total of 27 distinct instinctual variants. This exploration aims to illustrate the incredible complexity and richness of the Enneagram system.

Self-Preservation

People with a dominant Self-Preservation Instinct (Self-Pres, Self-Prez, or SP) are concerned with their well-being and the soundness of their bodies to meet their needs. As the world is more developed and less about survival, this instinct is usually preoccupied with physical comfort, resources, or things that provide security and safety (either physical or psychological). Sometimes this can involve finances, food, shelter, medical resources, and psychological safety. People with a strong Self-Preservation instinct are usually very in tune with what they need to feel safe, comfortable, and content. When functioning at average and healthy Levels of Development, they can extend that intuition outward and recognize the needs and desires of others. Self-Pres people can have vibrant social lives and satisfying partnerships. When their demands are not met, they can easily withdraw. This tendency can make Self-Pres types more introverted. Self-Pres individuals can be content with domestic tranquility and a secure and stable partner.

*grounded | practical | serious | introverted |
self-aware | sensible | introspective | protective*

Social

People with a dominant Social Instinct (SO) are preoccupied with how they are affected by and can maintain social connections and bonds with others. While the Self-Preservation instinct is concerned with affecting their environment, the Social instinct is more concerned with how they can adapt to fit into any social situation they may find themselves in. People with a strong Social instinct are highly attuned to how their actions and behaviors affect those around them and will adjust their approach to seek out personal connections. Social people will usually seek out strong relationships with others, attempt to maintain long-term bonds, and stay involved in their lives. Social people focus more on impacting their communities and environments than their other Instincts. They will seek out partners who will share in their social endeavors and can sometimes lose themselves in the vastness of other people's identities and desires.

warm | open | engaging | socially responsible |
interactional | extroverted | adaptable | flexible

Sexual

Individuals with a dominant Sexual Instinct (also known as the One-on-One Instinct) are primarily driven by a deep desire for intense energy and strong connections with others. It's important to note that when we use the term "sexual," we are not solely referring to seeking out sexual or physical experiences. But that is not to say that these experiences are disregarded or excluded. The Sexual Instinct encompasses a broader range of intense connections beyond just the physical realm. While the Social Instinct seeks to maintain connections with other people, the Sexual Instinct is different in that it constantly moves forward, seeking an intensity that will provide satisfaction and stimulation. People with a strong Sexual Instinct are more energized and outwardly motivated to have their needs met than the other Instincts. They move toward whatever will fulfill their desires or needs, and sometimes when those needs are not met, they will move on to find a new source of stimulation.

intense | aggressive | emotional |
extroverted | open | energized |
dynamic | outwardly motivated

Levels of Development

The Levels of Development established by Don Riso and Russ Hudson demonstrate the varying degrees of how each point can show up in the world based on presence. "Unhealthy," "average," and "healthy" refer to the Levels of Development and the overall state of a person's ability to function. The energy at each point can show up very differently depending on how healthy or unhealthy the individual is; this is a common reason why many people mistype or feel uncomfortable at their dominant point. The Enneagram Institute, founded by Riso and Hudson, perfectly sums up this concept:

> *The Levels of Development provide a framework for seeing how all of the different traits that comprise each type fit into a large whole; they are a way of conceptualizing the underlying "skeletal" structure of each type.... Further, with the Levels, a dynamic element is introduced that reflects the changing nature of the personality patterns. You have probably noticed that people change constantly. Sometimes, they are more explicit, more accessible, more grounded, and emotionally available, while at other times, they are more anxious, resistant, reactive, emotionally volatile, and less accessible. Understanding the Levels makes it clear that when people change states within their personality, they shift within the spectrum of motivations, traits, and defenses that make up their personality type.*

HEALTHY	**L1**	BEING	Freedom From Ego Structure
	L2	ALLOWING	Psychological Capacity ("I am")
	L3	DOING	Social Value/Gift
AVERAGE	**L4**	EFFORTING	Social Role/Imbalance
	L5	IMPOSING	Interpersonal Control
	L6	AGGRESSION	Overcompensation
UNHEALTHY	**L7**	VIOLATING	Violation
	L8	COMPLUSIVE	Delusion & Compulsion
	L9	DESTROYING	Pathlogical Destruction

The Levels of Development according to Riso and Hudson

❖ **Healthy:** becoming expansive and unconstricted in essence; fully present in the world

❖ **Average:** beginning to allow our egos to guide our behaviors; dropping into destructive patterns when we fall asleep to our true selves, with a fluctuation of presence

❖ **Unhealthy:** dysfunctional and destructive behaviors when ego becomes the driving force behind everything we do; falling into ego-based patterns that trap us in personality

THINGS TO REMEMBER

❖ There are nine points on the Enneagram map. We can access all the points but lead with one dominant energy. The numbers are not a scale, meaning no point is better or worse than any other points.

❖ No point or type is inherently gendered or dependent on dimensions of diversity (perceived race, socioeconomic status, education, age, religion, etc.). While the descriptions and energies of the points are universal and are not dependent on certain identifying factors, it is essential to note how an Enneagram energy can vary based on cultural or environmental influences or psychological well-being. For instance, some cultures have specific gender roles, socially acceptable values, or religious influences that can impact the Enneagram energy. Still, these factors do not fundamentally change a person's dominant Enneagram point.

❖ Your dominant Enneagram point does not change throughout your life or shift based on your home or work life. You are born into your point or type, and your experiences adjust how you navigate life, access your wing energy, travel with the arrows, and drop into the Levels of Development.

❖ No one can tell you where you stand on the Enneagram map. You find your place by reading, researching, and exploring all aspects of the nine points. Tests can help you narrow down the choices, and you may find your point or type by process of elimination. Tests are not always the defining factor of where you stand on the Enneagram map; the tests' quality matters.

❖ Many people mistype and thus spend years trying to find where they stand on the Enneagram map or try to fit themselves into whatever they want their dominant energy to be. Only some aspects of the point may apply or appeal to you; this does not mean you are mistyping. You may mistype, but there is wisdom in learning why you mistyped and what it means to connect to a specific energy that may not be your dominant point within the Enneagram. Explore the fundamental aspects of the Enneagram as defined above to help you dive into the complexities of your own personality. The last section of this book will help you find your Enneagram point. Remember: discovering where you fit within the Enneagram is a journey, not a destination.

As mentioned earlier, this book primarily provides a solid foundation for understanding the fundamentals of the Enneagram. So, we have outlined the many aspects of the Enneagram that require deeper exploration towards the end of the book. As you embark on your Enneagram journey, consider the information provided as a starting point to grasp how the Enneagram operates and to help you identify your own Enneagram point.

Part II

THE POINTS

Chapter 3

The Body Center
8-9-1

The Body Center, called the Instinctive or Gut Triad, is where Points Eight, Nine, and One reside. These three points are linked to the body's wisdom and gut intuition. While we all have wisdom in our bodies and a certain amount of gut intuition, for the Eight, Nine, and One, this energy is at the core of their actions, behaviors, and beliefs. The Body Center energy is focused on action—affecting the world or their environment to avoid being influenced, controlled, or limited by it, and expressing their anger or rage in different ways.

The instinctual motivation to protect or defend human survival resides within the Body Center. This is the center that "gets things done," because the Eights, Nines, and Ones are wired to take or value action more readily than most.

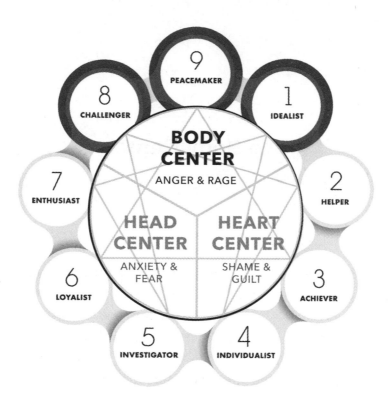

The Body Center of the Enneagram

The Wall of Anger and Rage

People who identify with the Body Center points have a distinct experience with the emotion of anger or rage. As a human being, it is natural to experience anger. However, for Body types, anger catalyzes many of their behavior patterns. During times of pain and suffering, either internally or externally, Eights, Nines, and Ones experience a visceral response that often transforms into bodily action, instinctual external or internal rage, and a deep desire to control, in one way or another, what is happening.

Many people within the Body Center experience a wall of anger and rage surrounding an unhealed or unexplored internal wound. This wall creates a barrier to accessing the authentic self; how it is addressed or ignored depends on the individual. For some Body types, the anger can stem from an early memory of feeling betrayed, rejected, ignored, unimportant, or not good enough. Each point deals with this barrier differently, but when we are stuck in a toxic pattern of behavior, the internal anger often transforms into an outward expression directed at others.

For Eights, anger tends to be a natural way of being and often doesn't feel like anger internally but is experienced externally by others very differently.

For Nines, the anger is often repressed and ignored until it cannot be held in any longer. Then suddenly, the anger erupts like a volcano, leaving pain and regret in its wake, internally and externally.

For the Ones, anger is usually not viewed as anger. Anger can be considered an inappropriate emotion—a loss of control, so to speak—and can feel like the One is admitting they've made a mistake. This is why many Ones don't honestly think they are angry. The repression of their genuine emotions festers from within and turns into resentment, eventually leaking out internally and externally.

We will explore this concept in-depth for each point later on in the book, but the main takeaway is that in the Body Center the anger and rage can be masking a much deeper issue.

Point Eight: *The Challenger*

Self-Confident, Decisive, Willful, Confrontational

*"I am good or okay if I am strong
and in control of my situation."*

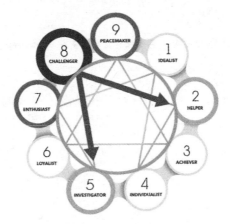

Basic Desire: To protect self with an appearance of strength and control

Basic Fear: To be harmed or controlled by others, to be vulnerable

Core Motivation: To maintain control and strength so as to not be vulnerable and risk being harmed by others, to demonstrate self-reliance, strength, and rejection of weakness, to dominate the environment, and to stay in control of all situations

Core Wound: Self-controlled—disconnection from the nurturing figure: *"I will take care of myself and be the strong one to prevent being harmed or rejected."*

TRADITIONAL ENNEAGRAM LANGUAGE

PASSION	FIXATION	VIRTUE
LUST	VENGEANCE	INNOCENCE

⬇ ⬇ ⬇

TRANSITIONAL ENNEAGRAM LANGUAGE

Manifestation of Suffering in Our Shadow Side	Pattern of Behavior When Trapped by Personal Challenge	Releasing Ego Agenda & Stepping into Essence of Being
a relentless search for a challenge, cause, or recipient of/for the intensity of an overabundance of energy	*a way of seeking out outlets for the angry energy, leading to the feeling that others must pay for betrayal or wrongdoing*	*a return to a pure heart by finding strength in vulnerability and power with rather than power over others, surrendering the egoic agenda opens heart to relinquish control and feel fully alive and free*

Examples of Eight Energy: Martin Luther King Jr., Kamala Harris, Toni Morrison, Alexandria Ocasio-Cortez, Winston Churchill, Indira Gandhi, Saddam Hussein, Donald Trump, Fidel Castro, G.I. Gurdjieff, Richard Wagner, Franklin D. Roosevelt, Lyndon Johnson, Mikhail Gorbachev, Golda Meir, John McCain, Pablo Picasso, Ernest Hemingway, John Wayne, Frank Sinatra

Wings

Eight has wing access to Point Seven and Point Nine

EIGHT WITH A NINE WING

AUTHENTIC SELF	SHADOW SELF
energetic	unable to control anger
confident	stubborn
protective	rigid
compassionate	emotionally detached
supportive	overly confident
able to see different perspectives	disregard for rules

EIGHT WITH A SEVEN WING

AUTHENTIC SELF	SHADOW SELF
logical	insensitive
makes fair decisions	callous
innovative and optimistic	disregards emotional honesty
inspirational	dismissive of others' feelings
decisive	unable to listen to others
engaged	combative and abrupt

"If you're going to hold someone down you're going to have to hold on by the other end of the chain. You are confined by your own repression."

TONI MORRISON

Lines & Arrows

Eight has lines with arrows that connect to Point Five and Point Two

EIGHT TO TWO

AUTHENTIC SELF	SHADOW SELF
receptive to vulnerability seen as a strength	easily offended
cultivating compassion	holding unrealistic expectations
caring and more open to connection	emotionally demonstrative
	manipulative
	belligerent
	dismissive

EIGHT TO FIVE

AUTHENTIC SELF	SHADOW SELF
emotionally controlled	isolated and withdrawn
anger becomes a wake-up call	detached from others
develop more caution	lacking in compassion
self-reflective	easily angered and provoked
gut reactivity is slowed	

"Darkness cannot drive out darkness; only light can do that. Hate cannot drive out hate; only love can do that."
MARTIN LUTHER KING, JR.

Summary

Andrew Carnegie said, "Immense power is acquired by assuring yourself in your secret reveries that you were born to control affairs." If you stand at Point Eight, power and control can be the catalyst for how you show up in the world. You have an innate drive to be in control and have power over yourself and everyone around you. Forceful energy resides within you, and how you utilize it to acquire or maintain control and power depends on your definition. Your need for control and power at Point Eight is rooted in preventing others from controlling you.

For some, control and power are ways to protect themselves from feeling vulnerable or what they may consider "weak." For others, control and power are ways to maintain boundaries from things that may physically and psychologically harm them. Eights actively resist being affected by their environment by clearly defining their control and power.

If the dominant energy you experience is at Point Eight, you are driven to exert tremendous force in the direction of everything you do. The unyielding state of intensity, strength, assertiveness, and ability to take charge and move forward is a normal way of being for people who stand at Point Eight. You may expect others to meet your level of intensity, but you are often left feeling disappointed and sometimes angry when the level of energy is not reciprocal. It is common for people who identify as an Eight to experience being seen as bossy, domineering, or overbearing. Even when manifested from a protective or well-intentioned place, the aggressive stance and powerful energy you embody may unintentionally have a profoundly different effect on people.

Conversely, your natural predisposition toward protecting others and standing up for your beliefs can place you in actual strength and leadership positions. When you are operating within healthy Levels of Development, you become gentler in your approach to conflict, and you can function from a place of compassion and kindness. You can access your vulnerable side and let people in to experience your immense capacity for friendship, love, and connection. This makes you a fiercely protective, loyal, and caring friend to many different types of people.

Levels of Development

Healthy

When operating within the healthy Levels of Development at Point Eight, you find strength through vulnerability and a return to the purity of an innocent heart. You can take action with compassion and empathy, leading others by example into a healing space.

You can become a defender from this place as you take a stand in safeguarding humanity. The emergence of your true spirit allows you to overcome the basic fear of being controlled or harmed by outside influences. You can surrender to the reality that you cannot control everything, and you harness your authentic strength as a selfless guardian and protector. As a healthy Eight, you can become one of the leaders who genuinely access their heart space and begin to operate from love and proper awareness in the face of divisiveness, confrontation, and conflict instead of attempting to confront the challenges with forged aggression. The surprising capacity for gentleness and love residing in the Eight energy is more potent than anyone expects.

Average

Most humans reside within these average levels and fluctuate up or down depending on the circumstances they find themselves in. As you drop down into the average Levels of Development, the ego agenda begins to take over. The fluctuations can create opportunities for you to pause and cultivate the presence you need to examine your thoughts and actions and course correct. This allows you to move up in the levels and avoid falling back into unhealthy patterns of behavior and thought. However, as the ability for honest self-reflection and course correction wanes you can become a hardened version of your authentic self, unwilling to allow your innocent heart and capacity for gentleness to emerge for too long. The fear of opening up and communicating with someone who may challenge your strength can bury your ability to find deep compassion in your big heart. You can express a wide range of emotions at this level, but a wave of underlying anger usually fuels your behaviors. You can become confrontational and egocentric—benevolent one moment and belligerent the next. A mixed bag of emotions and behaviors emerges: vindictive, protective, boastful, guarded, loyal, willful, insecure, and emotionally demonstrative. This broad range of expression can be intimidating.

You may share a common characteristic with other Eights at this level who feel uncertain about their surroundings, believing you must provide for and protect yourself. You build walls to keep everyone and everything at a safe distance until you are ready. The fear of betrayal and being let down by others can lead you to unleash a toxic energy of vengeance that alienates people and creates divides in many relationships. The opportunity to pause and engage in honest emotional reflection and objectivity becomes a struggle for you at this level. You may often react with forged strength and gut reactivity to conceal your vulnerability and capacity for gentleness. The anger and reactivity can morph into a wake-up call to step into a healthy space, or they can deteriorate into a toxic pattern of thoughts and behaviors. It takes a great deal of self-reflection and inner work to rise up through the levels and avoid dropping further.

Unhealthy

When unhealthy, you can become incredibly ruthless, unrelentingly cruel, vengeful, omnipotent, and highly destructive as you begin to justify your actions and beliefs from the unhealthy energy of Point Eight. Fear, anger, and control are the primary motivators that distort your reality, resulting in disdain for humans who may be perceived as a threat to your way of life. You become demonstrative in your cruelty and aggressively defend your beliefs to appear strong and in control. Deep down, what is being protected is your vulnerability and personal trauma. The fear of being in a weaker position can trigger a deep rage aimed at whomever or whatever is challenging your position of power. You may often find it difficult to address your internal wounds and trauma; fearing vulnerability, you will strike out and perpetually exert your energy with rage and a thirst for revenge.

Instincts

Self-Preservation Eight

As a Self-Preservation Eight, typically you may be more protective of your possessions and position and usually less sensitive toward the people around you than the other Instincts in Eight. At times it can feel like Five energy. You tend to be more practical and focused on securing your place as impactful and essential, which is how you manage your need for power and control. You set clear boundaries and work diligently to ensure your position of power is acknowledged and respected at home and work. As a Self-Preservation Eight, you are incredibly protective of your inner circle and will make sure others know who is in charge when challenges arise. The Self-Preservation instinct in Eight can create tension when connecting with others. It can also provide a supportive and protective atmosphere when others feel alone, unsafe, or vulnerable.

Social Eight

If you are a Social Eight, you tend to focus your energy on the bonds you create with others, often creating a circle of trusted friends you like to test from time to time, much like the energy of a strong-willed Two. Loyalty and trust are how you exert your power and control. You enjoy a good debate, but when you feel betrayed, you will drop anyone who you think is involved in this betrayal. You can hold grudges easily and will wield your control over your social groups to make sure your position is respected. As a Social Eight, you can be more aggressive in exerting your energy outward. You can come across as overbearing when engaging with new people or when in unfamiliar social situations. The

Social instinct in Eight creates long-lasting connections across all walks of life. These Eights can often be the glue that holds groups together.

Sexual Eight

If you are a Sexual Eight, your energy is focused much like the Sevens, in that you are usually spontaneous and can become easily bored with anyone who cannot meet your level of intensity. You enjoy a good time and can debate and argue with humor and lightheartedness. As a Sexual Eight, you lean toward finding partners and an inner circle that you can reshape and form into what you want. The powerful energy of a Sexual Eight is front and center at all times. This energy can make some people uncomfortable if you are unaware of how your presence affects the people around you. It is a challenge, especially if you are unwilling to adjust how you approach the person or situation. The Sexual instinct in Eight makes for an intensity that many can find unnerving, but people will often gravitate toward this energy without knowing it.

Challenges and Overcoming the Egoic Agenda

As an Eight you may project the appearance of an invulnerable human being who can maintain control of all things, but deep down, you guard your innocence and hinder your boundless compassion from flourishing. The deep fear of being controlled or harmed by external influences may cause you to construct walls around your big heart to protect yourself from being hurt and letting others in. Your vulnerability is a strength, not a weakness.

You often experience a need for control to keep yourself protected from whatever might render you vulnerable. This need for control constantly drives your actions and can be exhausting. Power with rather than power over others is a struggle you probably know all too well. It can feel uncomfortable to let go of control of your environment, including control over anything external that might influence your environment. You meet people with intense energy to test the boundaries you've created and assess their intentions, but this energy can push people away before you can connect with them. Your energy seeks ways to control the people and things around you, and you may not be aware of the real intention behind your actions. For instance, you may look for ways to help someone overcome a challenge, but instead of asking them how to help, you may assert yourself and decide what's best for them with little regard for what *they* need or want. Your actions are rooted in your desire to control, and until you have done more inner work, this may be challenging for you to explore further.

Be true to your authentic heart.

Don't hide it behind a brick wall.

The Path of Inner Work

The Eight's personal challenge or passion of lust, as it is taught in the Enneagram, is a deep desire to take on life with all of the energy you can produce. Your Point Eight energy seeks more of everything: challenges, control, action, intensity, and so on. The power that your Eight energy brings into everything matters and drives you to push the limits in your life, often landing you in no-win oppositional situations. This conscripted stance is the default to enforce power over whomever or whatever you perceive to be the adversary. Your unique way of navigating challenges can lead you to a thirst for revenge, a concept taught as the fixation of vengeance. This is where you get trapped, and your rage becomes the guidance for your automatic pilot. The dominant stance and reacting with a vengeful force are your ways of masking your Achilles heel: vulnerability. The invitation to move into a healthy space is attainable when you access the gift of reason at Point Five, moving away from the toxic emotions of rage, lust, and vengeance blocking your true heart. Enter the transformative space of the heart at Point Two, where you can rediscover your innocence, taught in the Enneagram as the Eight's virtue. From this place, you will reclaim your balance and peace to go into the world with authentic strength as a compassionate human being.

Responses to Conflicts

Unhealthy Reaction

Deep rage expressed outwardly at others and your surroundings; taking an uncompromising stance; intimidation; relentless aggression; destructive anger; insensitivity; "steamrolling" of others; fear of being "called out" causes irrational outbursts and intimidating language choices; resistance toward anything forced/imposed upon you; inability to access compassion; domineering stance intended to intimidate others into backing down; constantly looking for a challenge or conflict to channel whatever anger you are holding on to

Healthy Reaction

Pausing for reflection and slowing down gut reactivity; objective reasoning; finding compassion; a strong drive to protect the weak/vulnerable/mistreated/misunderstood; using your powerful stance, voice, and presence for those in need; staying a person of your word; standing up for what you believe in at all costs; natural-born leadership tendencies; unwavering courage, truth, and determination; authentic vulnerability in showing your softer side during conflict

Finding Your Place at Point Eight

We asked individuals to describe their Enneagram journey to help illustrate how the energy is expressed at each of the Enneagram points. Elita's journey represents Point Eight.

Eleven years ago I was invited to spend a weekend at the local meditation center here in Latvia. I was told that apart from meditation practice we would talk about "nine faces of your soul." I had never even heard the word Enneagram before. I believe it was one of the first Enneagram workshops here in Latvia.

I listened to descriptions of personality types with the utmost curiosity. However, for me, it was just another typology where I was supposed to find myself. We started with Type One. I liked it and, although we had been told that there were no better or worse types, I decided that Type One would be kind of superior to the others (since they started with it) and therefore would suit me well. I chose that type also because it felt like familiar and strong energy.

During the break, I told our teacher that I found my type and that was Type One. He asked me about my "inner voice." "What voice?" I replied in my big astonishment. "Nope, you are not Type One, if you do not know "what voice." It wasn't until the end of the following day when I discovered my true type.

We went through seven other types, and I almost lost my patience. Then we started to talk about bossy, pushy, straight-talking, domineering Type Eight. When I heard that Type Eight people tend to behave like "a bull in a china shop" without noticing how it affects other people, I instantly pictured one of my colleagues and held my breath in a big revelation— I finally knew what was wrong with that woman and why she was so extremely difficult to get along with.

While my mind was happily bouncing about my new discovery (I felt like I finally nailed her), something else was happening in my body. As the description proceeded, I started to feel nauseous. I blushed terribly, I got some kind of heat wave, and I could not look at the others because I was convinced they were looking at me. Because the story I heard was ALL about me. I felt totally exposed, even stripped.

Only at the end of the class, I experienced tremendous relief. I finally was diagnosed, and I knew what was "wrong with me," but the most important—my sickness was "curable." That was in February 2012.

A month later, in March 2012, I went to California to attend part one of the Enneagram training with Russ Hudson. I knew he was one of the best in this field, and I needed the best authority to surrender to. Everything had to be and was big for me at that time. I did not know yet that it was not really me; it was just my Eightness.

I could not believe how surprisingly accurate were these descriptions of my type (or of me as I thought then). "We are all programmed, predictable, and therefore controllable," I wrote home then. I spent hours and hours reading the Enneagram books and trying to find something "they still did not know about me" until Russ Hudson said, "You can spend lots of time trying to entertain yourself with more details about your type, or start working with your self-awareness right now, and make changes."

It did not take me long to discover my type, because it stood out so vividly. Every single detail in the story of Eights was about me. At that time, I was already quite self-considerate and self-aware. I had done my inner work through meditations, kriya yoga, reiki, etc., but I felt I was missing some guidance in my personal and spiritual development. I was looking for a mentor, a teacher in my life. The Enneagram as a profound teaching about nine personality types became such *a teacher to me. Only after I got introduced to the Enneagram could I start focusing on my inner and unique way of development through more focused and targeted self-observation as part of my inner work. It brought me into a new relationship with myself and the world. I am still using self-observation as a powerful method not only of self-study but also of self-change. Realizing the tremendous impact of the newly found information on my own life, I was trying to reach various groups of people in my nearest circle to raise awareness of how trapped we were in our behavior patterns and that we ought to be free.*

A few years later, I finished the training program for Enneagram teachers and got certified by the Enneagram Institute. I have been delivering Enneagram workshops and conducting one-to-one coaching sessions since. I am a co-founder of a professional theater where the Enneagram is one of my main tools in advising directors and actors on creating authentic characters. I use the Enneagram in my everyday professional life as CEO of a real estate development company, but the most important Enneagram is still the most loyal companion in my inner work. After all, if I want to teach anything to anybody, I have to remember that "a teacher can take her students only as far as she herself has gone."

During my journey over the last 10 years, I have learned to admit that my tough exterior hides a sensitive, loving, and devoted human being. It is my basic fear of being harmed or controlled by others that prevents me from showing my sensitivity and vulnerability to the world. When I practice my presence, I am different from many of these ideas about myself.

When I am present and my own type is relaxed, I start to feel things that are normally foreign to me— like tenderness, compassion, and receptivity. I use my power and strength to support and uplift others because I start to notice what other people actually need in order for them to be empowered. I am able to express my feelings in simple, sincere, and loving ways. I have to admit that most of this I have learned and experienced through my children. The innocent presence of my two daughters brought out the best in me, like gentleness, benevolence, forbearance. My response to them is completely sincere, direct, and heartfelt. If I could just learn to have these feelings for others, for everybody, at any time and any place.

My greatest current type-related challenge is to get back grounded in my body, because most of the time I am fixed in my mind settings. I realize that I have to be in my body to reach my heart, sensitivity, and vulnerability from there.

I noticed that when I am really opened to presence and really feel my body and my breath, my sensations, I start feeling more alive and filled with more energy and being less reactive. I feel powerful and sensitive at the same time, ready to do what I need to do and enjoy the whole thing. I am learning to be affected by life instead of reacting to it. I want to be touched by life in all possible ways and live it from my vivid alive energy, my realness and confidence, encountering kindness, my vulnerable feelings and sensitivity beyond what I am used to dealing with. I want to celebrate my existence in this amazing world and live my life from this confident aliveness, and the inner work is my vessel to get there, but I always "remember that you are not doing The Work: you are allowing The Work to be done in and through you," from the 12 Principles of Inner Work.

ELITA, LATVIA

REFLECTIONS FOR POINT EIGHT

❖ How do you resonate with the basic fear at Point Eight?

❖ How does the basic desire at Point Eight manifest for you?

❖ How do you resonate with the core wound at Point Eight?

❖ Consider the energy at Point Eight: What do you feel is missing from your being?

❖ What are you searching for?

❖ What does it look like when you feel out of control, vulnerable, or betrayed?

Point Nine: *The Peacemaker*

Receptive, Reassuring, Complacent, Resigned

"I am good or okay if I am at peace and those around me are good or okay."

Basic Desire: To find inner peace, maintain stability, and preserve harmony

Basic Fear: To experience loss and separation, to have inner peace and harmony disrupted

Core Motivation: To create harmony in your environment, to avoid conflicts and tension, to preserve things as they are, to resist whatever would be upsetting or disturbing to inner peace

Core Wound: Self-numbing—connected to both parental figures: *"I must withdraw and anesthetize myself to all conflict to keep my world from falling apart."*

TRADITIONAL ENNEAGRAM LANGUAGE

PASSION	FIXATION	VIRTUE
SLOTH	INDOLENCE	ACTION

⬇   ⬇   ⬇

TRANSITIONAL ENNEAGRAM LANGUAGE

Manifestation of Suffering in Our Shadow Side	Pattern of Behavior When Trapped by Personal Challenge	Releasing Ego Agenda & Stepping into Essence of Being
a deep state of denial and avoidance of all things: feelings, reality, challenges, hope, presence, humanity	*avoidance of external influences that may force an awakening to the pain, suffering, or anything that may be disturbing*	*find presence to recognize own strength and power and then take right action to bring peace and harmony to not only self but everyone*

Examples of Nine Energy: Barack Obama, Alicia Keys, Ronald Reagan, Colin Powell, Carl Jung, Abraham Lincoln, Gloria Steinem, Queen Elizabeth II, Joseph Campbell, Morgan Freeman, Dwight D. Eisenhower, Audrey Hepburn, Norman Rockwell, Gerald Ford, Walter Cronkite, Carl Rogers, Joseph Campbell, Walt Disney, Ron Howard, Gary Cooper, Jimmy Stewart, James Taylor

Wings
Nine has wing access to Point Eight and Point One

NINE WITH AN EIGHT WING

AUTHENTIC SELF	*SHADOW SELF*
willingness to fight for truth and justice drive to find solutions with strength and perseverance	inability to control anger rebellious confrontational aggressive and assertive when provoked

NINE WITH A ONE WING

AUTHENTIC SELF	*SHADOW SELF*
principled in finding harmony balanced perspective strong focus on helping improve lives of others ethical but fair and just	highly principled in maintaining rigidity passive-aggressive self-righteous judgmental deeply resentful

"Great leaders are almost always great simplifiers, who can cut through argument, debate and doubt, to offer a solution everybody can understand."
COLIN POWELL

Lines & Arrows

Nine has lines with arrows that connect to Point Three and Point Six

NINE TO THREE

AUTHENTIC SELF	SHADOW SELF
establish voice with confidence, value, and charisma	*easily overwhelmed*
actively seek out and maintain connections to others	*concerned with outside judgment*
	depersonalized
awakened sense of purpose	*cold and distant*

NINE TO SIX

AUTHENTIC SELF	SHADOW SELF
energetic	*scattered*
alert	*overwhelmed with fear/anxiety*
accountability	
responsibility	*indecisive and reactive*
driving motivators	*insecure*
reflective and focused	*outbursts of irrational anger*

"Whenever one person stands up and says, 'Wait a minute, this is wrong,' it helps other people do the same."

GLORIA STEINEM

Summary

"Change will not come if we wait for some other person or some other time. We are the ones we've been waiting for. We are the change that we seek." These words spoken by Barack Obama illustrate the complexities behind Nine energy. On the other hand, when pressed by a pushy reporter for an interview during his breakfast at a small diner in Pennsylvania, Obama replied, "Why can't I just eat my waffle?" This is the other side of Nine energy. If Point Nine is where you stand on the Enneagram map, the need to keep peace and find harmony is the driving force behind your actions and behaviors. In a world full of challenges and struggles, most humans try to find their own ways of resolving conflict, but for you, this may be a way of life. At Point Nine, the desire to control or maintain boundaries against anything that may harm you—in whatever form that may take for you—is rooted in a deep desire to not let anything affect your equilibrium or inner peace. For some, this energy is exerted internally and externally to resist anything that may penetrate their boundaries.

At Point Nine, the gaze is automatically drawn to finding ways to either avoid or resolve conflict; if you are a Nine, you have the ability to see the big picture and the many ways of addressing (or not addressing) situations. Stability, avoiding conflict, compromise, and mediation create your comfort zone. You have a strong drive to maintain balance and harmony, both internally and externally, in order to not feel loss or separation from whatever resides within your comfort zone. The filter through which you view the world around you is one of quiet internalization and sometimes repression of true feelings in order to not wake up to reality. You may be familiar with the feeling of being seen as complacent, indifferent, or apathetic. One of the biggest challenges for most Nines to gain access to the gift, or virtue, is the daily repression of your authentic selves in order to not feel anything that may affect your environment—passive-aggressive behaviors, saying yes when you really mean no, avoiding conflict to maintain a false connection with others, choosing to remain asleep instead of addressing the reality of life. Presence is the main obstacle for most Nines; presence in addressing your true feelings and beliefs, and your powerful impact on the world around you.

On the other side, your natural predisposition toward finding balance and harmony during conflict and a deep desire for maintaining the peace can place you in positions of true strength and purpose. When you are operating within the healthy Levels of Development, you become present to the sheer power behind your actions and your contributions to the world around you. You can maintain your presence during anything—even conflict—and connect with others using your calming and benevolent energy. This makes you a powerful and reassuring friend for many different types of people.

Levels of Development

Healthy

As a Nine operating within the healthy Levels of Development, you become an engaged and forceful leader. You are willing to face conflict with an unexpectedly powerful impact and a calm but present serenity. You become a fierce defender of humanity, a quiet but surprisingly assertive leader on the front lines of the battle for love, compassion, and reconnection. You navigate life through inner strength and the courage to honor your authentic self in the face of divisiveness, confrontation, and conflict. The need for maintaining inner peace and stability at any cost evolves into an externalization of finding peace and harmony for everyone through honest, reasoned, and harmonious approaches. You can take the right action and remain present without the fear of being affected by disruptive influences. You recognize the power of your voice in the face of challenges and step into a leadership role with courage and intentional presence.

Average

Most humans reside within these average levels and fluctuate up or down depending on the circumstances they find themselves in. As you drop down into the average Levels of Development, the ego agenda begins to take over. The fluctuations can create opportunities for you to pause and cultivate the presence you need to examine your thoughts and actions and course correct. This allows you to move up in the levels and avoid falling back into unhealthy patterns of behavior and thought. However, as the ability for honest self-reflection and course correction wanes, you begin to project a false sense of calm and you may fall into old patterns of "numbing out." You can become unwilling to engage authentically and begin to struggle with your ability to maintain your presence. You may become emotionally numb and self-effacing. You deflect the responsibility for honest reflection and accountability and can embrace a "go with the flow" mentality as you fall into passiveness. The "not my problem" outlook becomes a fallback, leading you down a path of denying or justifying your complicity in the widespread disconnection of humanity.

As you experience fleeting moments of awakeness, your true strength shines and you are a beacon of light in the storm. You may experience this flicker of hope when you begin to find presence, but it can be short-lived as you find the presence too disruptive to your routine of passivity. The anger and indolence can morph into a wake-up call to step into a healthy space or they can deteriorate into a toxic pattern of thoughts and behaviors. Presence becomes your main obstacle at this level. It takes a great deal of self-reflection and inner work to rise up through the levels and avoid dropping further.

Unhealthy

As you drop into the unhealthy levels, you can become deeply repressed, ineffectual, unquestioningly loyal, and painfully angry. You actively justify your actions and beliefs from the unhealthy energy of Point Nine. If you are an unhealthy Nine, you may be capable of embodying true apathy; becoming destructively cavalier, distant, unfeeling, or indifferent, you have a repressed anger lurking within a cold and detached exterior. Anger and denial are the primary motivators that distort your reality, resulting in a disdain for humans who may disrupt your inner peace or force you to wake up to or acknowledge your anger. As an asleep Nine, you may feel hopeless in the face of challenges and change and often revert to a level of numbness that allows your inner peace to remain falsely still. Unhealthy Nines can often be found among the masses of the unquestioning and complacent, unwittingly attaching themselves to anything that lets them release their anger even if it is misdirected or unrelated. If you fall into the unhealthy levels of Point Nine, you can become so detached from humanity that you develop a complete disregard for basic human decency. Presence is a true challenge; when you neglect the importance of your inner voice and bury your true emotions, you remain too stubborn to "wake up" and deal with reality.

Instincts

Self-Preservation Nine

If you are a Self-Preservation Nine, you tend to be more easygoing and complacent, often finding comfort in the simplicity of life, more so than the other Instincts in Nine. You are likely to be quieter and more reserved in regard to your connections with other people and situations. Finding inner peace in your routines and ability to "zone out," you can lean into apathy as a means of coping with your anger and anxiety around not living up to your own expectations. You may have a hard time stepping out of your comfort zone to meet new people or create new experiences, but you are willing to go with the flow when you are surrounded by people you know or with whom you feel a level of comfort. The Self-Preservation instinct in Nine can create a barrier when connecting with other people, but it can also provide the harmony and stability many people search for in a trustworthy friend or loyal partner.

Social Nine

As a Social Nine you may focus your energy outward on creating and assimilating into peaceful and harmonious groups of companions and families. You tend to be more outgoing and flexible in your approach to connection and ability to find inner peace. In creating a clearly defined place within your group or family you often lose sight of what you really want or need and feel anxious or angry about your lack of personal development, similar to an unhealthy Two. Much like the energy of a Six, you can have a tendency to merge your life with others, even in toxic environments, as long as you can find comfort and stability in the group. The Social instinct in Nine creates a welcoming and comforting energy in any group and many people will gravitate toward this energy when they feel uneasy or need a calming presence.

Sexual Nine

If you are a Sexual Nine, you are likely more focused on creating strong bonds with another person or persons. You use your energy to fuse with another person, often merging with the other person's emotions, beliefs, desires, and so on, which feels similar to the energy of Two. As a Sexual Nine, you probably have a more defined relationship with your anger as it is easily recognizable and expressed when your connections are jeopardized, much like the powerful energy of the Eight. Unlike the other variants within the Nine, as a Sexual Nine you might not have a problem with understanding and expressing your emotions. However, you typically find it difficult to define who you are outside of the person or persons with whom you have attached yourself. The Sexual instinct in Nine can create tension when connecting with other people outside of close relationships, but to other people the intimate Nine energy is both calming and unexpectedly stimulating at the same time.

Challenges and Overcoming the Egoic Agenda

As a Nine you may appear to be calm, cool, and collected on the outside, but your seething anger, indifference, and repression of self-worth are forcing you into a false state of inner peace. The deep fear of having your equilibrium disturbed in one way or another may cause you to repress your true emotions and feelings, leading you to believe that it won't matter anyway. Your passive stance and seemingly lackadaisical apathy say more than you think, especially during conflicts that may arise. When you allow your anger to wake you up to your own voice, you can use that energy to propel you into action. Your voice and presence become a force to be reckoned with—people will listen, engage, and feel seen by your surprising power.

You often fall into patterns of complacency during times of conflict, which can cause you to fall asleep to yourself and the true depth of your powerful presence in the world. The repression of your true self can cause a wave of deep and torturous anger to build within you. Your energy seeks to control and maintain your boundaries against anyone or anything that may affect your equilibrium or your inner peace. This stance can manifest as apathy and result in a disconnection from the ability to maintain presence. For instance, you may avoid asserting yourself during moments of conflict, whether you can see a solution or not, and harden the boundaries you establish. Your actions are rooted in your desire to control your environment, and until you have done more inner work, this may be a challenge for you to explore further.

There is a world of difference between waiting to see how things play out and being present to the reality that it is time to intervene.

The Path of Inner Work

The Nine's personal challenge, or passion of sloth in the Enneagram, supports your deep desire to remain unaffected by reality and the challenges you may face in the hope of maintaining a false sense of inner peace. Your energy seeks to avoid anything that may challenge your ability to numb out or to cope with the demands of your feelings and the feelings of others. The inactivity that your energy can foster is a destructive pattern of behavior intentionally designed to deny you the ability to engage in life and live up to your full potential. Your acceptance of a delusional approach to life is a concept taught as your fixation on indolence. You get trapped in this space and your anger and apathy become the guidance for your automatic pilot. You protect yourself from being disrupted or forced to wake up by running away from challenges, often seeking superficial solutions to detach from being held accountable for your actions. There may be a sense of fatigue when you become overwhelmed or disheartened by the current state.

The invitation to move into a healthy space is attainable when you access the gift of objective reasoning. Use clear focus to address your true feelings at Point Six. Move away from anger, sloth, and indolence as they are duplicitous emotions that are blocking your true heart. Enter the transformative space of the Heart Center at Point Three, where you can harness your ability to take action, taught in the Enneagram as the Nines' virtue. You will reclaim your balance and strength to remain present through anything.

Responses to Conflicts

Unhealthy Reaction

Passive-aggressive behaviors; avoidance of issues; denial; repression; "numbing out"; self-effacing attitude; deflection; extreme dissociation; "volcanic" outburst of repressed/misplaced anger; unresponsive to someone in need; complete disregard for basic human decency when faced with difficult situations that may force you to wake up to your anger and pain and acceptance of a delusional approach to life; to protect yourself from being disrupted or forced to wake up, you run away from challenges, frequently seeking out easy solutions to detach from being held accountable for your actions, leading to a sense of fatigue when you become overwhelmed or discouraged

Healthy Reaction

Pausing for reflection and finding the strength of your presence; taking action; forcefulness; engagement; passion; supportive with purpose; open and receptive to ideas while maintaining universal truths; strong drive for peace and harmony bolstered by right action; kindhearted approaches; genuinely caring; down to earth; easygoing mentality; generally calm; persistent; loyal; dedicated to a cause

Finding Your Place at Point Nine

We asked individuals to describe their Enneagram journey to help illustrate the expression of the energy at each of the Enneagram Points. Tom's journey represents Point Nine.

I was invited by my wife in Norway many years ago to attend a one-day Enneagram presentation. I didn't know what the Enneagram was; I had never heard about it, and my wife had heard about it but didn't know anything of the content, the origin of it, or what it was about. I decided to go anyway, and the Norwegian trainer started by presenting Point One on the circle. I felt for every type he went through that I was that type. I really could associate and identify myself in being the various points along the circle in all of the Enneagram. So I was kind of confused during the day, and when he finally got to number Nine, it sort of clicked in for me. I felt like it was coming together from all the other types and that they were all included in Type Nine. That's what I thought. I felt so proud of being the best of the types, with all those wonderful qualities and attitudes. Peacemaker!

The presenter, Kjetil Hauge, had translated a book by this German author, Andreas Ebert, which we later read and discussed, but unfortunately, we didn't see the implication of getting to know our type. Years passed, and I forgot about it. Then finally we found out that there was another presentation, and I was invited again by my wife and we went. From that time on it became apparent to me that this was actually a way to get to know myself better and to get a better grip on my life. At that time I was rather frustrated by my ego trips. I kept doing things that I didn't want to do, like commenting and being funny with people, being what I thought was humorous, but I actually offended and made it difficult for people around me. Among many other things in my being, I needed a way to change. The more I learned about myself and my Type Nine shadow behaviors, I became both shocked and embarrassed. At times I was so ashamed and bewildered. I hated my Type Nine. I honestly hoped the Enneagram might help me in doing change work.

I found my type because I felt a strong connection to the Type Nines wanting world peace. I hate conflict.

Another important point is that I find myself a slow thinker. When talking, I tend to talk slowly, with several detours, before I finally arrive at a possible conclusion. I am formulating meaning and opinion as I speak. I am, in some ways, not taking advantage of social settings in joining the conversation by sharing my views. I couldn't find my own position on a certain topic. On another issue, let's call it red, I would see the good things and bad things in the red, and if another came up with an opposing position, let's call it blue, I also see the advantage and the disadvantage in blues. So I went back and forth between red and blue while listening to the other person's position in the conversation. At the time I might have found out my position, I might have discovered that purple would be a position I could identify with. And at the time, I wanted to state my view and present the various possibilities of the red and the blue, and the conversation had sort of waned; by the time I found my purple position, the conversation on that issue was already over and they were on to the next topic.

When facing a serious difficulty, I tend to look at it from a positive angle. If something unpleasant happens, I can easily turn the difficulty around and see the positive prospect in that difficult position.

When conflict arises, I think it will pass, and if I stay quiet, people may leave it, or the heated energy will go out of the conflict. Maybe the conflict might solve itself if enough time passes. So instead of going head-on into the conflict, I tend to wait for it to solve itself. Over and over again, I notice that I tend to add to the conflict by not going into a conflict and not challenging the unpleasantness of taking action.

I see myself as a nice, easygoing person. I do like to listen to people. I like asking questions to have them define their position and feelings. Being the listener and one that asks questions makes me feel connected, which is very important to me. I'm curious, and I like to get to know people, not the superficial side of them but the way they think, feel, and reveal their qualities. I tend not to share my thoughts and feelings until I'm invited to, or at least I feel that they want to listen and get to know me. Then I do love to talk about myself. If I'm in a group setting and I'm finally charged to find my place and be active in the conversation, I enjoy myself and sense the energy. In social settings, I can stay quiet for a long time and just smile and be nice. I might also be thinking about my own things and not actively engage in the conversation. I've found out later in life that when I do that, I'm really being perceived as positive. At the same time, I might actually create conflict by not stating my position, not stating what I want, not asking for anything, not demanding anything, and the people present get frustrated and insecure about me, unsure of where I stand.

I've heard from people over the years that Type Nines are lazy. I do not feel that I am lazy when I'm really invested in a project, and working hard and long hours. I have gotten burned out at least two or three times in my life, so I don't see myself as lazy, but I have found that the laziness of my type has been that I do not bother to use the energy to find out what I want the most. Over the years I never found an answer to the question of what I wanted to be when I [grew] up. I retired without knowing. I chose an easy education path in life. I sort of have gone along with what came along. I've changed careers a couple of times because I was invited by others, and I almost never actively [sought] out the career change myself. I haven't really taken on the difficult process of finding out what I really want, so I've ended up just getting along and saying yes to invitations. I have a really hard time saying no socially, but more importantly, I have a really hard time saying yes to myself. I spent a lot of energy trying to please people to make myself feel included and be a natural member of a group. I've done that by using my bodily sense to feel other people's needs and try to make them happy and at the same time want them to include me. My greatest fear is to be left out and to have the feeling of being excluded, not having contact, not being reckoned with, and not having worth.

By being lazy in this way, I have the feeling of having wasted my talents, energy, and many opportunities in life when I did not take the effort to find out what I really wanted. This truth really made me sad thinking of all the years I could maybe have used my talents more in tune with my true needs and my own wants.

When I recognize and define my goals and put my focus on them, I really feel much better, with huge energy, at home in my body and it makes me happy.

At this last stage of my life as I retire, I have the opportunity to use more time for silence and inquiry. I find myself less defensive in my relationships with people around me. This is an effect of having acknowledged more of my shadow sides. Whenever I find out that I have underperformed, I am now more aware of my tendency to cover up my feeling of shame by idealizing, by allowing myself to stay truthful.

I have this strange connection to John Lennon's song "Imagine." It really reconnects with my deep feeling and belief in world peace. Every time I hear that song it makes me crack up and I cry because it really resonates with my values. I really believe, like John Lennon, that we would have another world if we could really experience "the brotherhood of man" where we are all equal, across nations, across cultures, and I do think that would be a path to world peace. My active engagement in working with the Enneagram is truly a tiny, tiny, tiny contribution from my side in trying to achieve world peace.

Tom, Norway

REFLECTIONS FOR POINT NINE

❖ How do you resonate with the basic fear at Point Nine?

❖ How does the basic desire at Point Nine manifest for you?

❖ How do you resonate with the core wound at Point Nine?

❖ Consider the energy at Point Nine: What do you feel is missing from your being?

❖ What are you searching for?

❖ What does it look like when you feel detached, angry, or asleep to your true nature?

1

Point One: *The Idealist*

Principled, Purposeful, Self-Controlled, Perfectionistic

*"I am good or okay if I am good
and do what is right."*

Basic Desire: To have integrity, to be good, virtuous, to do the "right thing," to live up to the ideal of ethical and moral perfection

Basic Fear: To be wrong or make a mistake, to be corrupt or unethical, to cause harm to others, to be inappropriate or feel defective

Core Motivation: To strive higher, improve everything and everyone, to be consistent with ideals, to justify self, to be beyond criticism so as not to be condemned by anyone

Core Wound: Self-judgment—disconnection from the protective figure: *"I must self-correct and heed the punishing voice of my inner critic or I will cause harm."*

TRADITIONAL ENNEAGRAM LANGUAGE

PASSION	FIXATION	VIRTUE
ANGER	RESENTMENT	SERENITY

TRANSITIONAL ENNEAGRAM LANGUAGE

Manifestation of Suffering in Our Shadow Side	Pattern of Behavior When Trapped by Personal Challenge	Releasing Ego Agenda & Stepping into Essence of Being
an internalized fury aimed at anything that challenges the idea of right or good, or anything that points out own flaws; typically unable to acknowledge the anger at all	*actively engage in directing anger and judgment toward others to avoid acknowledging the reason for anger, outward channeling of inner rage and criticism*	*acceptance of the imperfections of life by accepting what is instead of "what should be" while maintaining a pure definition of integrity and a genuine moral compass*

Examples of One Energy: Mahatma Gandhi, Pope John Paul II, Nelson Mandela, Michelle Obama, Margaret Thatcher, Osama bin Laden, Prince Charles, Rudy Giuliani, Kate Middleton, Jimmy Carter, Al Gore, Hillary Clinton, Justice Sandra Day O'Connor, Dr. Jack Kevorkian, Martha Stewart, Ralph Nader, Jerry Seinfeld, Bill Maher, Tina Fey, Katherine Hepburn, Maggie Smith

Wings

One has wing access to Point Nine and Point Two

ONE WITH A NINE WING

AUTHENTIC SELF	SHADOW SELF
calm approach to conflicts	redirect emotions or avoid emotions entirely
peacemaking tendencies	
balance and harmony	detachment
	inflexiblity
	stubborness

ONE WITH A TWO WING

AUTHENTIC SELF	SHADOW SELF
deeply connected to helping	self-righteousness
advocates for others	criticism aimed at others
supportive and sensitive	frustrated and controlling
warm and caring	manipulative
	judgmental

"You must not lose faith in humanity. Humanity is an ocean; if a few drops of the ocean are dirty, the ocean does not become dirty."

MAHATMA GANDHI

Lines & Arrows

One has lines with arrows that connect to Point Seven and Point Four

ONE TO SEVEN

AUTHENTIC SELF	SHADOW SELF
balanced and joyful	disregard
open-minded and relaxed	impulsive
ability to adapt and become flexible	fault-finding
	judgmental
	scattered and unfocused

ONE TO FOUR

AUTHENTIC SELF	SHADOW SELF
deeply connected to compassion	self-absorbed
emotional honesty	deeply judgmental
ability to internalize anger	harsh criticisms
appreciation for other perspectives	hypocritical behaviors
	moody and detached

"Our human compassion binds us one to the other—not in pity or patronizingly, but as human beings who have learnt how to turn our common suffering into hope for the future."

NELSON MANDELA

Summary

"As long as poverty, injustice, and gross inequality persist in our world, none of us can truly rest." These words, spoken by Nelson Mandela—arguably one of the most notable and inspirational Enneagram Ones in history—sum up what it's like to stand at Point One on the Enneagram map. As a One, it's likely you have a strong calling or mission that guides you in everything that you do, and more often than not you strive for perfection and absolutes in almost every area. At Point One the gaze is automatically drawn to what is wrong; you can intuitively see what needs fixing or improvement. The lens through which your world is viewed is one of constant need for improvement, self included. You want to make the world a better place and sometimes it is overwhelming. Ones actively resist allowing their environment to affect them or to breach their boundaries by clearly defining the parameters by which they live their lives. For some, the persistent control over their actions and behaviors is a way of maintaining a life that appears to be virtuous/ethical/good/righteous so as to not allow anything to breach their self-righteous bubble. For others, the clearly defined parameters of their world prevent anything that may tempt them into betraying their values or doing something that may cause harm to breach their inner sanctum.

If you stand at Point One, you undoubtedly have a strong drive to abide by a moral compass and a need to live up to your principles by controlling how you protect yourself from your environment. Integrity, a strong sense of purpose, and a need for order and justice create the comfort zone for you at Point One. Dualistic concepts are more appealing for you as they lend themselves to removing complexities and shades of gray. When things are black or white, good or bad, the choices lend themselves to being contained to decisions that are more likely to be right. More often than not this leads to a relentless inner critic that pushes you to do better, to fix whatever may be "wrong," and to live up to an impossible standard you've set for yourself and ultimately one in which you impose upon other people.

The experience of being seen as cold, controlling, and judgmental may not be an uncommon experience for you at Point One. Even if your actions are well-intentioned, you may be unaware of the harmful impact of your words and behaviors. The constant need to critique, fix, or point out flaws may come from a well-intentioned place, but for people on the receiving end, it may be unwelcome, intrusive, judgmental, and harsh. On the other side, your natural predisposition toward making the world a better place and doing what is right for all of humanity places you in positions of true strength and leadership. When you are operating within the healthy Levels of

Development, you become flexible in your ability to find perspective and approach the world with an open heart and a desire to make things better through love and compassion. You become a person full of joy and gratitude for the complexities of life all while maintaining your drive to make things better for everyone. This balance of spontaneity and determination makes you a truly amazing friend for many different types of people.

Levels of Development

Healthy

In the healthy Levels of Development, you demonstrate a willingness to exercise reason, kindness, flexibility, and hope when faced with division, confrontation, and conflict. You have found serenity in the imperfections of life by accepting "what is" instead of "what should be" while maintaining a pure definition of integrity and a genuine moral compass. You become flexible in your approach to finding solutions and communicating across differences. People are no longer objects; you are able to move past polarities and treat other humans with dignity and respect instead of judgment and resentment. You are truly magnanimous and altruistic in your search for integrity, justice, and respect for all humans. As a healthy One you become virtuous, ethical, flexible, accepting, fair, objective, practical, compassionate, empathetic, understanding, willing to compromise or negotiate, balanced, philanthropic, benevolent, highly principled, and connected to true integrity.

Average

Most humans reside within these average levels and fluctuate up or down depending on the circumstances they find themselves in. As you drop down into the average Levels of Development, the ego agenda begins to take over. The fluctuations can create opportunities for you to pause and cultivate the presence you need to examine your thoughts and actions and course correct. This allows you to move up in the levels and avoid falling back into unhealthy patterns of behavior and thought. However, as the ability for honest self-reflection and course correction wanes, you can become emotionally constricted when you are only looking at situations through your own lens. On the downside, the experience of Ones is that of a more opinionated, moody, judgmental, stubborn, and angry individual. You can become intrusive and unable to listen to opposing perspectives. In an attempt to live up to your ideals and do good out in the world, you begin to hold impossibly high standards and get frustrated when things don't meet these standards.

As you experience fleeting moments of presence and growth, you can also feel an underlying current of resentment beneath many of your behaviors and feelings. In less healthy states, it is possible to become a judgmental individual who harbors significant anger towards oneself and others, with no one escaping this judgment. This anger may transform into resentment towards anything that highlights mistakes or challenges your moral values. In this position, you can lash out in a hypercritical but polite way to redirect the blame onto other people to maintain a false sense of integrity. You can use these moments of reflection as a wake-up call to step into a healthy space or allow them to deteriorate into a toxic pattern of thoughts and behaviors. It takes a great deal of self-reflection and inner work to rise up through the levels and avoid dropping further.

Unhealthy

As you drop into unhealthy levels, you become a self-righteous, deeply judgmental, inflexible, and cruel individual. You actively justify your actions and beliefs from the unhealthy energy of Point One. You may become a vessel for hatred and resentment, harshly judging anyone and anything who challenges your moral compass. This can trigger the defense mechanism of reactive formation, in which you develop contradictory actions and behaviors in order to hide your true emotions and beliefs. This paradox leads to a deep internal anger that corrupts your ability to see people as people, and instead you view them as objects. Anger, fear, and control are the primary motivators that distort your reality, resulting in resentment for humans that do not fall in line with your ideals. You become extremely pedantic and cold, and almost everything you do is mean-spirited. You are unwilling to compromise or listen to new perspectives, and you become unkind and deeply resentful.

Instincts

Self-Preservation One

As a Self-Preservation One you are more concerned with your material well-being and tend to be more self-controlled and critical than the other Instincts in One. You often worry about making mistakes and tend to see things in binary terms: good and bad, right and wrong. A mistake in your eyes could be your undoing, so you strive to control your life in regard to how you behave, what you eat, what you do and do not do, and so on. You may also place these standards onto others around you and become overly involved or judgmental when others don't value these things in the same regard. You can resemble Seven energy in your desire to indulge in experiences, but your strict inner critic quickly shuts down anything that may affect your self-control. As a Self-Preservation One you can drop into unhealthy Four energy when you begin to question how deserving you are in regard to enjoying things that make you happy—this is true concerning physical things, but also in terms of enjoying fun or rewarding experiences. The Self-Preservation instinct in One can create some tension when connecting with others, but can also serve as an inspiration for others to aspire to take better care of themselves and those around them.

Social One

If you identify as a Social One, you probably have a strong moral compass that guides you to serve as a crusader for the betterment of the world around you. You have high standards and want to see these same standards upheld in others and in society as a whole. You utilize your commitment to integrity and doing what is morally right to uphold your beliefs, often engaging in prolonged arguments and debates. You tend to be excessively critical and inflexible in your convictions, particularly when you feel that your integrity is being questioned or undermined. As a Social One you use your belief systems as a boundary against the world and against anyone that may compromise your claim to self-righteousness. The Social instinct in One places you in a position to connect with others in the hope of inspiring them to be the best they can possibly be, as long as you are willing to tap into Seven energy and find comfort in flexibility and balance.

Sexual One

As a Sexual One you tend to focus your energy on your personal relationships, especially your partner. You use your incredibly high standards to create an "idealized" relationship and will push your partner to meet your standards. Similar to the Social instinct in One, you will use your drive for goodness and righteousness to encourage your loved ones, friends, and family to be "the best version of themselves," but you usually don't extend that energy outward past your primary ring of connection. You can resemble Four energy in your pursuit of idealizing a relationship and finding a deep emotional connection with another person or persons, but you will repress and distort your feelings of envy or jealousy. Unlike the Four who will romanticize the other person or persons creating an internal image of desirability, you can become hypercritical and look for places where the other person is falling short. The Sexual instinct in One creates an internal tension of repressed emotions and a longing to fulfill the desire for connection. As a Sexual One, you can resemble Seven energy with a deep longing to fulfill intense desires, but like the other Instincts in One, you tend to refrain from indulging too much and always want to control yourself. When healthy, you can create an atmosphere where people strive to become the best they can be and feel comfortable connecting to you on a deeper level.

Challenges and Overcoming the Egoic Agenda

Your composed exterior is masking a seething anger aimed at everything that you see as a challenge to what you deem right/correct/good. The deep fear of being wrong or causing harm may amplify your constant search for perfection or for seeking out what is wrong in order to correct it. This imbalance can cause you to impart your own values, beliefs, and ideals onto other humans with little regard for the true impact of your good intentions, which leaves you frustrated and resentful.

The world is full of possibilities, and your idea of what is right may not be the case for someone else, and that is OK. The counterproductive practice of holding on to rigid polarities and becoming resentful and judgmental when things don't follow your specific guidelines of good and right is only causing harm to you and those around you. Your view of the world is filtered through a constant need for improvement, self included. The improvement and correcting of others are done in the spirit of "getting it right," though others may not view it as such. Often, the constant need for improvement, sometimes seen as a quest for perfection, is imposed upon others without regard for whether or not they desire or even need fixing, which can come across as intrusive, unwelcome, and controlling. Your energy seeks out a way to control the people and things around you, and you may not be aware of the real intention behind your actions. For instance, you may look for ways to improve a situation or correct someone by placing your own set of values and standards on them, sometimes with little to no regard for what *they* consider right or good. Your actions are rooted in your desire to control, and until you have done more inner work this may be a challenge for you to explore further.

Resist the urge to lead with a reprimand.

Acknowledge the good and course correct with kindness.

The Path of Inner Work

As a One your personal challenge, or passion of anger as it is called in the Enneagram, is the combination of your compelling desire and futile attempt to right all of the wrongs in an imperfect world. Your One energy seeks out mistakes, opportunities for improvement, and corruption. From your point of view, the constant drive to fix things can create disconnects when communicating and interacting with people. Your unique way of navigating challenges can lead you to a perpetually critical stance, sitting as judge, jury, and executioner; a concept that is taught as the fixation of resentment. This is where you get trapped and your anger and judgment become the guidance for your inner critic and automatic pilot. This hypercritical position and the subsequent judgments and assessments you place on other people is your way of deflecting the gaze from your own imperfections or shortcomings. The invitation to move into a healthy space is attainable when you access the gifts of emotional honesty and internal reflection at Point Four, moving away from anger, resentment, and judgment, as they are toxic emotions that pollute your true heart. Enter a transformative space by accessing the energy at Point Seven, where you reclaim your serenity, taught in the Enneagram as the One's virtue. This is where you will find true emotional balance, flexibility, and joy in the possibilities of life.

Responses to Conflicts

Unhealthy Reaction

Repressed anger; self-righteousness; rigidity; irritability; unfair/irrational criticism; avoiding emotional response out of fear of appearing improper/imperfect to others; displaying judgment/blame/prejudice toward others' demonstrations of anger/fear/injustice; severe judgments while rationalizing your own unhealthy behaviors; inability to access compassion; holding on to polarities of right and wrong; intolerance; absolutism; obsessive drive to fix whatever you deem wrong; live in a constant state of resentment and suppressed anger aimed at the world's faults; may experience a moment of empathy and understanding toward people in similar situations, but the fear of having your integrity or ideals questioned shifts you into a reactive state where you can justify your behaviors and actions

Healthy Reaction

Flexibility; serenity; hope; kindness; intentional pause for reflection; reactivity is slowed down; inspiration through compassion; ability to connect body/heart/head for a balanced approach to conflict; polarities are dissolved and perspective becomes more important than holding on to ideals; people are no longer objects; ability to move past polarities and treat other humans with dignity and respect instead of judgment and resentment; truly magnanimous and altruistic in your search for integrity; justice, and respect for all humans; become an outspoken powerful leader of true change and have a way of making everyone else see the path to joining causes to fight social injustice; resentment and anger evolve into a wake-up call to find balance when faced with challenges

Finding Your Place at Point One

We asked individuals to describe their Enneagram journey to help illustrate how the energy is expressed at each of the Enneagram points. Point One is represented by Tracy's journey.

I was introduced to the Enneagram archetype framework by Dr. E some years ago and she

recommended I purchase The Wisdom of the Enneagram *by Don Riso and Russ Hudson to learn more. And thus, my journey began. I was first drawn to taking the Riso-Hudson QUEST, the Quick Enneagram Sorting Test, to help me narrow down the possibilities of my type. Through this process, I resonated with both Seven and Three. I continued on the path of exploring both, and based on my usual optimism, desire for freedom, career accomplishments, and ability to pick up and go (seven relocations over a 20-year period), I landed on Type Seven. Also during this time, I completed a second assessment through a different organization that also resulted in Type Seven. It was not until I witnessed a panel discussion on all of the Enneagram archetypes that I began exploring Type One. It was as if a mirror appeared and I was standing in front of it when I heard the Type One panelists answer questions.*

I was fascinated by the existence of a framework that could expose my core psychological issues, interpersonal strengths and weaknesses, and also provide effective ways to deal with it all. As I discovered my dominant personality archetype at Point One, there were times when I was brought to tears as I realized how harsh and judgmental I must have been over the years toward people I care deeply about. It was also quite apparent for me that my constant desire to live a life of purpose influenced many of my major life transitions.

I have become quite aware of what is "right" and "wrong," especially as it relates to other people's behavior compared to what I deem is "right." When I observe myself in this pattern of thinking, I can sometimes accept the imperfection of humanity and release my judgment. This usually happens when I am more present in the moment—where there is no right/wrong or good/bad. Only the oneness of all humanity exists—we are all interconnected in our imperfections. I have also begun to release my desire and need for perfection. The inner critic is still there, but not as loud, as I move into acceptance of all aspects of myself and others.

I am now on the journey of exploring my relationship to all of the feelings and emotions tied to anger. I am accustomed to tamping it down, since displaying anger is not the "right" thing to do. What do healthy expressions of anger look like for me? As I explore feelings of anger that I deem are wrong or inappropriate, can I accept both the light and shadow sides of my personality? And, more importantly, how do I use the feelings of anger as a springboard to action?

TRACY, NEW YORK

REFLECTIONS FOR POINT ONE

❖ How do you resonate with the basic fear at Point One?

❖ How does the basic desire at Point One manifest for you?

❖ How do you resonate with the core wound at Point One?

❖ Consider the energy at Point One: What do you feel is missing from your being?

❖ What are you searching for?

❖ What does it look like when you feel angry, critical, or judgmental?

Chapter 4

The Heart Center

2-3-4

The Heart Center, also referred to as the Feeling Triad, is the center where Points Two, Three, and Four reside. The capacity for emotions and human connection can be linked to these three points. While we all have emotions and can create connections with other human beings, for the Two, Three, and Four this energy is at the core of their actions, behaviors, and beliefs. The Heart Center energy is focused on emotions, self-image, and value—determining their identity and the value they place on their self-identity plays a key role in how these three points show up in the world.

The acknowledgment and understanding of who we truly are and the value we feel reside within the Heart Center. In its purest form, every energy has access to the Heart Center and can experience true appreciation for our authentic selves—seeing our value beyond what others think of us. The compassionate approach to connection and kindness also resides in the Heart Center. These are the points that can access the heart space more readily because they are wired to tap into true emotion.

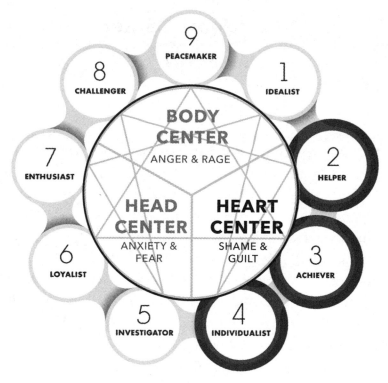

The Heart Center of the Enneagram

The Wall of Shame and Guilt

People who identify with the Heart Center points have a distinct experience with the emotion of shame or guilt, more so than the other centers. All humans experience shame and guilt; this is an undeniable fact. However, for Twos, Threes, and Fours shame is the catalyst for many of their patterns of behavior. During times of pain and suffering, either internally or externally, Heart types experience an emotional response that often transforms into internalized shame and redirected guilt. This pattern consequently bonds Heart types to the experience of emotions and connection. The Heart Center is concerned with their own self-identity and the method by which they defend or project this image to others. The hostility, defense, and shame around how they show up in the world are dependent on how the point in question is attempting to find their true selves, fulfill the core motivation, and avoid the basic fear.

Many people within the Heart Center experience a wall of shame surrounding a particular unhealed or unexplored internal wound—often involving how their presence shows up in the world. This wall creates a barrier to accessing the authentic self, and the method in which it is addressed or ignored is dependent on the individual. For some Heart types, the shame can stem from an early memory of feeling unwanted, unworthy, unseen, or not good enough. Each point deals with their shame differently, but when we are stuck in a toxic pattern of behavior, the shame we feel internally is often transformed into an outward expression aimed at redirecting our emotions onto others in one way or another.

For Twos, the shame is often redirected onto others and channeled into cultivating love. Their feelings of unworthiness propel them into finding outlets for them to be valued.

For Threes, the shame is usually repressed or denied entirely and projected outward as a shield to mask any feelings of unworthiness. Shame is not an emotion many Threes are willing to admit or deal with.

For Fours, the shame is internalized, renamed, and held on to as a method of finding their identity and establishing value. Fours are unique in that they don't mind the darker side of their guilt and shame and often they can transform it into something else.

We will explore this concept in depth for each point later on in the book, but the main takeaway is that in the Heart Center the shame and guilt can be masking a much deeper issue.

Point Two: *The Helper*

Generous, Caring, People-Pleasing, Possessive

*"I am good or okay if I am loving
and I am close to others."*

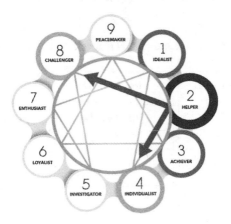

Basic Desire: To be loved, needed, and wanted by others

Basic Fear: To be unlovable, unneeded, and unwanted by others, to be unworthy of love

Core Motivation: To strive to be lovable, to express feelings for others, to be needed and appreciated, to get others to respond, to vindicate claims about self, to be seen as a generous and caring person

Core Wound: Self-sacrifice—ambivalence toward protective figure: *"I must earn love through selfless acts for others and repression of self needs or I will be unlovable."*

TRADITIONAL ENNEAGRAM LANGUAGE

PASSION	FIXATION	VIRTUE
PRIDE	FLATTERY	HUMILITY

⬇ ⬇ ⬇

TRANSITIONAL ENNEAGRAM LANGUAGE

Manifestation of Suffering in Our Shadow Side	Pattern of Behavior When Trapped by Personal Challenge	Releasing Ego Agenda & Stepping into Essence of Being
the formation of a love-worthy appearance on the outside to mask an internal sense of being unlovable	*seek out connections to feel valued and manipulate true emotions in the hopes of being seen as indispensable and worthy of love/attention*	*acceptance of authentic self allows for a deeply unselfish and humble human who is free to give to others with abandon, generosity, and no strings attached*

Examples of Two Energy: Mother Teresa, Maya Angelou, Bishop Desmond Tutu, Eleanor Roosevelt, Mr. Rogers, Nancy Reagan, Danny Thomas—founder of St. Jude's, Tammy Faye Bakker, Marlo Thomas, Monica Lewinsky, Leo Buscaglia, Richard Simmons, Luciano Pavarotti, John Denver, Lionel Richie, Stevie Wonder, Barry Manilow, Dolly Parton, Bill Cosby, Sally Jessy Raphael

Wings

Two has wing access to Point One and Point Three

TWO WITH A ONE WING

AUTHENTIC SELF	SHADOW SELF
aware of own growth	*self-critical*
encouraging	*seeking approval*
supportive	*insecure*
deeply connected to helping	*uncomfortable*
advocates for others	*judgmental*

TWO WITH A THREE WING

AUTHENTIC SELF	SHADOW SELF
adaptable	*overly competitive*
communicative	*obsessive*
self-aware	*manipulative*
flexible	*dishonest*
highly responsive	*difficulty taking care of own needs and well-being*

"We ourselves feel that what we are doing is just a drop in the ocean. But the ocean would be less because of that missing drop."

MOTHER TERESA

Lines & Arrows

Two has lines with arrows that connect to Point Eight and Point Four

TWO TO EIGHT

AUTHENTIC SELF	SHADOW SELF
anger used as wake-up call to find truth and strength	deeply angry
	belligerent of others who do not value them
compassionate	distorted emotions
loyal and fiercely protective	
powerful	manipulative behaviors

TWO TO FOUR

AUTHENTIC SELF	SHADOW SELF
deeply connected to compassion, empathy, and emotional honesty	self-absorbed
	deeply judgmental
find inner voice	self-centered behaviors
self-aware	manipulative
takes care of own needs	sad and moody

"We are each made for goodness, love and compassion. Our lives are transformed as much as the world is when we live with these truths."

BISHOP DESMOND TUTU

Summary

If you haven't been living under a rock over the past 40 years or so, you have probably heard of *Mr. Rogers' Neighborhood*. Mr. Rogers reminded us that "knowing that we can be loved exactly as we are gives us all the best opportunity for growing into the healthiest of people." If only we could all be a little bit more like Fred Rogers the world might be a kinder place. Mr. Rogers and the energy of his entire "neighborhood" is the epitome of the Enneagram Two. He taught us to love one another but also taught us we need to love ourselves. If you stand at Point Two, this concept is not unfamiliar to you. Love is at the center of all you do. The reasons behind your love and the love you seek can be a tricky web to untangle. Two energy is warm and kind, but it often comes with strings attached. Regardless of how you give and receive love, the reasons behind your actions are usually rooted in the need to feel worthy of love in some form so that you can clearly identify yourself. It is a need to be seen and embraced by the outside world. For some, the need to form a strong self-identity is a way of maintaining a sense of pride around being a good and decent human who is worthy of love. For others, the clearly defined self-identity that is being projected is a way of masking low self-worth and manipulating the way people view them.

If the dominant energy you experience is at Point Two, you may have an innate drive to help others. In order to ensure that you are loved and needed by others you may employ whatever strategies you can to meet the mark. When we use the term love here, it is not only in the traditional sense of showing affection for someone, it is also in the deeper sense of wholeness and unity; love is a state of being, a sense of connectedness to one another. You have a strong drive to help, and you seek out places where you can offer support and a caring approach to challenges.

Kindness, compassion, and the need to develop connections create the comfort zone for you at Point Two. This energy is relationship oriented—though not necessarily romantic—and can sometimes manifest in manipulative or people-pleasing ways. The need to create and maintain connections drives you to go out of your way to sustain the dependencies in other people that you have created. The experience of being "the one person people can count on" or not having the ability to say no is not uncommon for you at Point Two. Even if your actions are well-intentioned, you may be unaware of the destruction you leave behind when you create dependencies in which people feel validated in their own toxic behaviors or dependencies. At the same time, what you consider helping may actually be harming when you fail to follow through with authentic compassion and truth. On the other side, when you are able to move past people-pleasing and manipulative behaviors, your true worth shines through; you become genuinely selfless and deeply connected to other humans. When you are operating within the healthy Levels of Development you tap into the natural ability to help others whenever and however they need it without manipulation or a hidden agenda, and you seem to have a capacity for pure love and light beyond what most people experience. This energy makes you a loyal, protective, and truly irreplaceable friend for many different types of people.

Levels of Development

Healthy

When operating from a healthy level of development, you can embrace your authentic self and understand that you do not need to conform to what you "should be" in order to gain love, have value, or create connection. You are unapologetically true to your own beliefs and operate from a pure heart full of compassion and genuine empathy for others in the face of divisiveness, confrontation, and conflict. You recognize your own needs as valid and important and can take care of your well-being while still extending your compassionate energy outward to others. The force of your inner strength guides you to choose spaces where you can support, lead, or create change from a purely good heart with no hidden agenda.

Average

Most humans reside within these average levels and fluctuate up or down depending on the circumstances they find themselves in. As you drop down into the average Levels of Development, the ego agenda begins to take over. The fluctuations can create opportunities for you to pause and cultivate the presence you need to examine your thoughts and actions and course correct. This allows you to move up in the levels and avoid falling back into unhealthy patterns of behavior and thought. However, as the ability for honest self-reflection and course correction wanes, you can become people-pleasing, emotionally demonstrative, condescending, flattering, and codependent. At this level, you may seek out connections to feel valued, and you can manipulate true emotions in the hopes that people will value you for what you offer and not for who you truly are. In this space, you can become manipulative, overbearing, placating, coercive, reticent, self-deceptive, presumptuous, and guilt-ridden. The guilt and shame at these levels can morph into a false sense of pride and distorted self-worth and cause you to drop further down the levels. You can use these moments of reflection as a wake-up call to step into a healthy space or allow them to deteriorate into a toxic pattern of thoughts and behaviors. It takes a great deal of self-reflection and inner work to rise through the levels and avoid dropping further.

Unhealthy

As you drop into the unhealthy Levels of Development, shame, guilt, and manipulation become the primary motivators that distort your reality resulting in your self-inflicted suffering and a deeply selfish campaign of seeking out validation or sympathy for your "efforts." You become a highly manipulative, self-serving individual who plays the victim card to pull people into your pity party in the hope of gaining sympathy and reassurance that you are loved. Blaming everyone around you for your own wrongdoing, all the while never seeing the depth of your manipulations, you become deeply disconnected from your authentic self and your true heart.

Instincts

Self-Preservation Two

If you are a Self-Preservation Two, you can be more focused on serving others as a way of securing a reciprocal relationship where you feel others will meet your needs. You tend to take pride in your sacrifices, often clinging to a martyrdom mentality. Two energy often has difficulty tending to individual needs; as a Self-Preservation Two you may be more in tune with what you need to maintain your well-being as it pertains to your ability to take care of others. You may experience a distortion of compensating for your generosity by demanding attention from others for all you have sacrificed for the people in your life. You are incredibly giving and helpful, oftentimes taking care of everyone around you, whether it's cooking for them or helping them through difficult times in some way or another, but you will overextend yourself to the point of exhaustion. When healthy, you can see when this is happening and sometimes can shift into a more self-aware approach to navigating challenges. The Self-Preservation instinct in Two can create some disingenuous behaviors when connecting with others but can also provide a deeply supportive and protective atmosphere when others feel alone, hurt, or in need of kindness and compassion.

Social Two

As a Social Two you focus your energy on the bonds you create with others, often becoming "the friend everyone can rely on." You enjoy being the center of a large group of friends and can connect many different types of people with your warmth and generosity, which makes you resemble Seven energy. This outward energy can come at a cost, however, as you will not accept being overlooked or unnoticed as you get lost in the friend group you have created. Much like Three energy, you want to be seen and garner attention for your efforts and will not hesitate to manipulate people or situations to create dependency. By offering advice, sometimes unwanted and intrusive, you find a way into other people's lives and can become patronizing and enable toxic behaviors in others. However, the Social instinct in Two can establish long-lasting bonds that connect people across all walks of life, much like Eight energy, as long as you remember to move past your hidden agenda and find humility and strength in your own self-worth.

Sexual Two

If you identify with the Sexual instinct of Two, you tend to focus your energy much like the Four, in that you are usually drawn to one person and want to cultivate a deep and intimate bond with this person. In *The Wisdom of the Enneagram*, Don Richard Riso and Russ Hudson refer to the Sexual Two as "the true intimacy junkies of the Enneagram." You enjoy finding a way into another person's life by connecting with them through things the other person likes, such as music, movies, hobbies, and so on. You may find a partner and cultivate a small group of a few close friends that you focus much of your attention toward. Unlike the Social and Self-Preservation Instincts, as a Sexual Two you may actively keep your friend groups separated to ensure you have a secure position with everyone and will not be excluded from any group or situation. You can have trouble respecting boundaries and may become pushy and fall into inappropriate patterns of behavior when you begin to feel disconnected from others. The Sexual instinct in Two makes for an intensity that many can find intrusive, but more often than not people will gravitate toward this energy without knowing it. When healthy, you can cultivate an authentic and deep emotional connection and provide warmth and affection to many different types of people.

Challenges and Overcoming the Egoic Agenda

The deep guilt or shame you carry around your own self-worth can block your ability to access your authentic self and strip you of your humility. While radiating an energy that manifests the appearance of a selfless person, your distortion of self-worth challenges the very thing you live by: love and compassion. You may seek out opportunities to serve people "in need" but fail to follow through authentically when you realize there is no reciprocation of the energy you have invested. Your justification becomes a self-serving excuse of false martyrdom, which is entirely manipulative and hollow. Distortion and manipulation are roadblocks you encounter when you let your ego take over.

If you identify with Point Two, you may resonate with the experience of not being able to say no easily— you reject your own feelings or needs in order to shift focus externally and feel valued and appreciated by others. When operating from an unhealthy space, the energy of the love you project can sometimes be tainted by a hidden agenda; creating dependencies allows you to feel valued and worthy but can lead to toxic and manipulative behaviors. The challenge, if you are a Two, is noticing when manipulation and shame are affecting your ability to access true compassion and stifling your inner strength to find value in your own beliefs. Your actions are rooted in your desire to define, project, and defend whatever identity you need to feel worthy and lovable, and until you have done more inner work this may be a challenge for you to explore further.

The love that you truly need resides deep inside.

Give yourself the gift of finding it.

The Path of Inner Work

The Two's personal challenge, or passion of pride as it is called in the Enneagram, is the formation of a love-worthy appearance on the outside to mask an internal sense of being unlovable. Your Two energy seeks outlets for your boundless love to create a sense of value and a place in other people's lives. The connection that your Two energy brings into everything matters and drives you to push the boundaries of integrity and emotional honesty. This conscripted stance is the default to ensure you feel valued and worthy of love, even if it comes at the cost of your true self. Your unique way of navigating challenges can lead you into people-pleasing and hollow behaviors, a concept that is taught as the fixation of flattery. This is where you get trapped and your guilt and shame become the guidance for your automatic pilot. The manipulations you construct are not only hurting you, they are also fostering environments for toxic beliefs and behaviors to flourish, unchecked and thriving. The invitation to move into a healthy space is attainable when you access the gift of beneficial and helpful anger and inner strength at Point Eight, moving away from guilt, pride, and flattery, as they are misleading emotions that are blocking your true heart. Enter the transformative space of the Heart Center at Point Four where you can cultivate your humility, taught in the Enneagram as the Two's virtue. This is where you will reclaim your strength and emotional honesty and be able to go out into the world with a pure heart, ready to make the world a better place with love and compassion.

Responses to Conflicts

Unhealthy Reaction

Manipulation; flattery; inability to access authentic compassion; emotional distortion; shame; misdirected anger; claiming false martyrdom; playing the victim to gain attention and sympathy; distorting the truth to fulfill a need to be needed; emotionally demonstrative displays aimed at people who challenge your identity of being a good/loving/caring/generous person; vindictive or vengeful behaviors can arise as you drop into the lower Levels of Development

Healthy Reaction

Pause for honest reflection; courage; compassion; empathy; emotional honesty; genuine desire to help with no hidden agenda; develop the humility that comes with self-worthiness so that you can connect with others beyond disingenuous manipulation and find the inner strength as a fierce guardian of love; acknowledge healthy boundaries to manage honest reactions during conflict; using your healthy anger as a warning system and wake-up call to find the inner strength to honor what you really believe and then take the right action

Finding Your Place at Point Two

We asked individuals to describe their Enneagram journey to help illustrate how the energy is expressed at each of the Enneagram points. Point Two is represented by Kelly's journey.

I was participating in a women's leadership group, and the facilitators suggested that I would benefit from studying the Enneagram. They described the Enneagram, including the benefits of personal growth.

It sounded very promising, so I asked them what they thought my Enneagram type might be. They were reluctant to tell me, but after prodding them, they told me they thought I was a Two. I asked them to describe the Two and I immediately identified with the traits.

Shortly afterward, I attended a workshop with Russ Hudson. I did not take a test immediately, but when I did my results seemed to validate my assumptions about my Two energy.

When I was in the workshop with Russ Hudson, and he described Type Two, I think I was in tears most of the time. I had a better understanding of myself, including why I sacrificed myself for others, and why I did not take care of my own needs. I began looking at my life through this new filter, and I was shocked. I always thought I had free will, but this new awareness was teaching me that I was asleep when making most of the decisions in my life, especially relationships.

Since discovering my type, I have immersed myself in learning more about the Enneagram through workshops and books. I became more aware of my sense of self/ego structure and how it was part of my identity. I think the biggest benefit has been a deeper understanding of the nature of my personality. By practicing awareness, I am able to clearly observe my tendencies and make better decisions about how I extend myself and how I navigate my need to connect to others.

I continue to educate myself, and I'm connected with a beautiful community of people who understand the Enneagram, and provide me with an opportunity for reflection. There are always more layers to uncover, but I feel like I've worked through the hardest part of seeing myself as who I was created to be. I was told it will be a long journey and it is. I continue to practice presence to be aware of my body, heart, and mind. To be present during discomfort, to breathe, and to know that something else will arise, something else will be revealed.

Many of my old wounds have surfaced and begun to heal. And the armoring that I had built around me is slowly melting away. At times, I catch myself giggling at some of the old patterns that persist. I give them a little "thank you, I got this" and let them fade away. This brings me so much joy that I am no longer asleep to these conditioned reactions. I honor my feelings as they arise and seek out the reasons behind my reactions. My life is more alive and I am discovering my true essence. Each day brings more understanding, guidance, power, love, and authenticity. I am grateful for the Enneagram and the transformation that it has made in my life.

KELLY, CALIFORNIA

REFLECTIONS FOR POINT TWO

❖ How do you resonate with the basic fear at Point Two?

❖ How does the basic desire at Point Two manifest for you?

❖ How do you resonate with the core wound at Point Two?

❖ Consider the energy at Point Two: What do you feel is missing from your being?

❖ What are you searching for?

❖ What does it look like when you feel unloved, manipulative, or angry?

3 Point Three: *The Achiever*

Excelling, Adaptable, Driven, Image-conscious

"I am good or okay if I am successful and others think well of me."

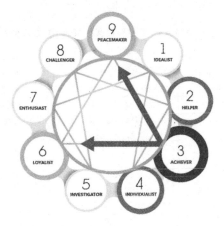

Basic Desire: To feel valuable, worthwhile, to be successful and admirable

Basic Fear: To be a failure, to feel worthless and of no value, to be unsuccessful, to feel deficient

Core Motivation: To be affirmed, to distinguish self from others, to have attention, to be admired, and to impress others, to appear worthy for what is accomplished in order to hide low self-worth/poor self-image

Core Wound: Self-rejecting—attachment to nurturing figure: *"I must earn love through my achievements and being successful or I will be useless."*

TRADITIONAL ENNEAGRAM LANGUAGE

PASSION	FIXATION	VIRTUE
DECEIT	VANITY	TRUTHFULNESS

⬇ ⬇ ⬇

TRANSITIONAL ENNEAGRAM LANGUAGE

Manifestation of Suffering in Our Shadow Side	Pattern of Behavior When Trapped by Personal Challenge	Releasing Ego Agenda & Stepping into Essence of Being
a constant drive to present self in a way that does not reflect authentic self but instead creates a mask of value, worthiness, and admiration	*seek out opportunities to prove self-worth by manipulating the truth to serve the internal drive to succeed and thus reinforce image of value*	*embracing of authentic self and acceptance of love and validation outside of external admiration and manufactured self-image; ability to move out into the world with honesty and authenticity*

Examples of Three Energy: Oprah Winfrey, Marianne Williamson, Brené Brown, Will Smith, Deepak Chopra, Bill Clinton, Jesse Jackson, Mitt Romney, Bernie Madoff, Candace Owens, Tony Robbins, Beyoncé, Muhammad Ali, Meghan Markle, OJ Simpson, Michael Jordan, Tiger Woods, Lance Armstrong, Elvis Presley, Paul McCartney, Madonna, Sting, Whitney Houston, Jamie Foxx

Wings

Three has wing access to Point Two and Point Four

THREE WITH A TWO WING

AUTHENTIC SELF	SHADOW SELF
dedicated	self-centered
self-aware	focused on image
efficient in making things happen	possessive
deep concern for people	unintentionally manipulative
warm and caring	

THREE WITH A FOUR WING

AUTHENTIC SELF	SHADOW SELF
adaptable	overly competitive
connected to others	egotistical
strive to improve self and others	manipulative
emotionally aware	emotionally distorted
receptive to others	act with hidden agenda

"We must go beyond the constant clamor of ego,
beyond the tools of logic and reason, to the still,
calm place within us: the realm of the soul."
DEEPAK CHOPRA

Lines & Arrows

Three has lines with arrows that connect to Point Nine and Point Six

THREE TO NINE

AUTHENTIC SELF	SHADOW SELF
ability to pause for reflection and emotional honesty grounded in the moment presence in order to grow	aimless and apathetic detached from compassion and self-awareness overwhelmed stressed

THREE TO SIX

AUTHENTIC SELF	SHADOW SELF
deeply connected to finding solutions release need to manipulate situations reflective honest	self-absorbed highly indecisive anxiety and fear take over impostor syndrome

"Authenticity is a collection of choices that we have to make every day. It's about the choice to show up and be real—the choice to be honest, the choice to let our true selves be seen."

BRENÉ BROWN

Summary

Oprah Winfrey once said, "Being human means you will make mistakes. And you will make mistakes, because failure is God's way of moving you in another direction." If you stand at Point Three, how you define and cope with failure can determine how you show up in the world. You have an innate drive toward success, and this energy is palpable to the people around you. It is likely you are an impressive human with a long list of professional, financial, family, or personal accomplishments. The reasons behind the internal motivation you feel to be successful—in whatever form that may take for you personally—can often be traced back to how you are trying to define your identity to the outside world. There is often a repressed feeling of needing to be someone who is worthy of love *just for being who you are*. This internal image you've created can lead you to intentionally design your life around this ideal persona so that you become the person you think is worthy enough. As a Three, you are constantly trying to define your self-worth through the identity you have constructed.

If your dominant energy resides at Point Three, you may feel compelled to achieve and prove your value through how you are perceived by others. Success, hard work, impressiveness, dedication, and ambition are just a few of the many extraordinary characteristics you may embody. Like many Threes, you probably have a strong aversion to the word *failure*. Failure in any form is directly opposed to the Three's essence of being. You are driven by determined and industrious energy, but it comes at a price: stay true to the authentic self or feed the ego. While the natural impressiveness associated with the energy at Point Three is almost always front and center, the polarity that must be managed is the way in which you obtained your success.

At Point Three, you are always aiming for the top—falling or failing is not an option. As you navigate challenges, you may cut corners or bend the truth to make sure you secure your position at the top. But this aversion to failure, in whatever form it may take, deprives you of opportunities to grow and become a whole human being who is authentically exceptional and capable of true greatness. In your search for success and achievement, you often forget to look back and offer a hand to those behind you. You become narcissistic, and your scope of focus narrows; you forget to honor your own humanity, thus negating everyone else's humanity along the way. On the other side, your Three energy can have a profound effect on those around you; your natural tendency to strive for being the best you can be inspires others to do better or be better. When you are operating within the healthy Levels of Development you become less concerned with being seen by others as the best, and your approach to life becomes more genuine from a place of self-love that you can easily extend outward.

Levels of Development

Healthy

As a Three operating in the healthy Levels of Development, you become self-accepting, authentic, modest, and charitable. You can use self-deprecatory humor to make people feel comfortable and at ease if they are intimidated by your truly impressive gifts. A fullness of heart emerges, and you are no longer afraid of dealing with true emotions as they arise. You become gentle and benevolent, leading with authenticity and inspirational charisma. You are willing to face failure with principled strength and resilience, leading with kindness and selflessness in the face of division, confrontation, and conflict. When healthy you have found truthfulness in the ability to access your authentic self and take right action with a collective awareness rather than a self-centered approach. You oftentimes will find worthy causes and channel your energy into making the cause successful and impactful, sometimes finding a supporting role without needing to be front and center. The need to project a "desirable" identity in order to maintain validation transforms into the emotional awareness for growth over progress.

Average

Most humans reside within these average levels and fluctuate up or down depending on the circumstances they find themselves in. As you drop down into the average Levels of Development, the ego agenda begins to take over. The fluctuations can create opportunities for you to pause and cultivate the presence needed to examine your thoughts and actions and course correct. This allows you to move up in the levels and avoid falling back into unhealthy patterns of behavior and thought. However, as the ability for honest self-reflection and course correction wanes, you can begin to project a fraudulent self-image; unwilling to engage authentically, you become shape-shifting and apathetic toward other people. In some cases, you can become conceited and self-serving, eventually deflecting your authentic self and repressing your capacity for true greatness. The drop in the levels can lead you to become emotionally stunted and make it difficult to align the connection between heart and head, almost as if there were a faulty wire. Moments of reconnection flicker, and you are able to access the space for reflection you need to reassess your thoughts and behaviors, but it becomes a challenge. You are apprehensive of forward progress or sacrifice without the guarantee of success; your hesitation is caused by fear of failure.

Often a hurt or insecure individual who feels that you must be "on top" to be valued—never overshadowed or outdone by others—you can become deceitful and dishonest, bending your truth to become whatever will make you the most "impressive." Your self-image becomes interwoven with how you are perceived by others and may not actually represent your authentic self. Impostor syndrome can become a recurring theme for you as you fluctuate within the average Levels of Development. The guilt and shame at these levels can morph into a combination of deceit, vanity, and low self-value and cause you to drop further down the levels. You can use these moments of reflection as a wake-up call to step into a healthy space or allow them to deteriorate into a toxic pattern of thoughts and behaviors. It takes a great deal of self-reflection and inner work to rise through the levels and avoid dropping further.

Unhealthy

When you drop into the unhealthy levels, you become extremely egotistical, self-centered, dishonest, vindictive, and duplicitous. You begin to justify your destructive actions and behaviors from the unhealthy energy of Point Three. You can also become relentless and obsessive about destroying whatever reminds you of your own shortcomings and failures. Fear, shame, and low self-worth are the primary motivators that distort your reality, resulting in a destructive arrogance that facilitates the dehumanization and dismissal of anyone who challenges your value. Deep down you fear that someone has seen through your facade and knows how much shame you are holding on to, which can trigger feelings of deep guilt and worthlessness. This only reinforces your aversion to failure, which will further fuel deceitful and narcissistic behaviors.

Instincts

Self-Preservation Three

If you are a Self-Preservation Three, you are typically focused on working hard to ensure your security and stability, much like the Enneagram Six. You tend to maximize your efforts in career growth and financial stability as a way of proving to others that you have value and are worthy. You will strive for success, recognition, and advancement in your career or social standing, which makes you a high achiever. Another way of looking at it is being a workaholic who controls your well-being with financial and material gains, much like Eight energy. You probably have a very hard time taking it easy, slowing down, or relaxing when you are forced away from work or achieving your goals. You may neglect relationships and family obligations, not because you do not care but because you view your success as a way of proving your worth to others. You're likely detail-oriented and fastidious in different areas of your life, much like One energy, but unlike the One you may not adhere to a moral compass and instead strive for achievement by any means necessary. The Self-Preservation instinct in Three can create some challenges when connecting with others but can also provide an inspirational energy for others to work harder or find the motivation to emulate your Three energy. As a Self-Preservation Three you can have difficulty prioritizing relationships over your achievements, but when healthy you can establish a balance and create deep relationships where everyone feels valued and uplifted.

Social Three

As a Social Three you can focus much of your energy on your status as a way of establishing a clearly impressive role in your social circles, much like Eight energy. You may rely on recognition and reassurance that you are not only impressive but that others see you as an inspirational person. As you become ingrained in your social groups you may feel anxious to prove above and beyond that you are at the top of your group in terms of finances, degrees, recognition, titles, material assets, or whatever resonates with you personally. This outward energy can come at a cost, however, as you will not accept being second best or being outdone in any way, much like Two energy in terms of seeking validation and attention. You can feel the need to brag about yourself, name drop, indulge in an exaggeration of your achievements and success. However, the Social instinct in Three can produce a truly inspirational person that elevates an entire friend group or social circle, as long as you remain present and humble enough to stay connected and grounded in authenticity.

Sexual Three

If you identify with the Sexual instinct in Three you may focus your energy on becoming the "human ideal" as you define it. You enjoy being admired and will strive to be incredibly impressive, alluring, and desirable, much like Sexual Two energy. You want to be desired, and you want other people to acknowledge that you are desirable. You will find partners and cultivate a small group of a few close friends, but unlike the Two, who focus their attention on other people, the attention is drawn inward as you use your alluring qualities to bring people closer to you. As a Sexual Three, you oftentimes have trouble admitting that you feel unworthy and the fear of connecting emotionally makes you establish boundaries with other people. While radiating a magnetic energy, you can also repel people as you begin to feel uncomfortable with your own emotions and deeply repressed shame. The Sexual instinct in Three makes for an intensity that many can find intimidating, but more often than not people will gravitate toward this energy without knowing it.

Challenges and Overcoming the Egoic Agenda

As an Enneagram Three it is highly likely that you have the outward appearance of a truly astonishing human being capable of incredible things. Underneath this impressive exterior, however, you are probably battling impostor syndrome and some strong feelings around being a failure. The deep fear of being seen as / feeling like you are worthless or a failure in some way drives you to fully embody anything that makes you feel worthy and gain acknowledgment and validation. This may cause you to neglect your true emotions, beliefs, and desires as you strive to maintain your paragon status.

You may feel a constant need to project an impressive exterior but deep down you are tiptoeing on the line of being truly great and being fearful that you are not, in fact, anything great at all. It is likely that you know the experience of impostor syndrome, as do a lot of people who identify with Three energy. You may believe that someday someone will see through your shiny exterior and discover that you are a fraud who is empty and undeserving. This fear leads you to conceal your true self and develop an impressive persona to mask whatever shame you are feeling about being loved for *what you do* instead of *who you are*. You must overcome this fear and step into your true potential with the confidence and acknowledgment that you do not need to be what others expect of you and that you can honor your authenticity with Grace.

Your greatest achievement will always be
how well you give and receive love.

The Path of Inner Work

The Three's personal challenge, or passion of deceit, as it is called in the Enneagram, is a deep desire to manifest an impressive image to mask your true self and prove you are a worthy human being. Your Three energy seeks ways to cultivate and develop your image in whatever form serves you best. The ambition that your Three energy brings into everything matters and drives you to push the limits in your life and in your integrity. This conscripted stance is the default to project and adapt an image that will garner respect, validation, and admiration. Your unique way of navigating challenges can lead you to repress your authentic self and leave you projecting a fraudulent image of yourself, a concept that is taught as the fixation of vanity. This is where you get trapped and your shame and the preservation of your self-image become the guidance for your automatic pilot. The deep desire to project a superior and impressive image to others leads you to believe that you must avoid failure at all costs. Your internal dialogue might fall along the lines of *if I fail, I am not worthy...if I am not worthy, what am I?* The projection of an impressive exterior is your way of masking your Achilles' heel: self-worth. You have built an impressive exterior but underneath you are a bundle of insecurities and a repression of your true self. You may believe that if people don't see you for what you do then they will have to judge you for who you are, and deep down you may be afraid of being undeserving of love. The invitation to move into healthy space is attainable when you access the gift of stillness at Point Nine, moving away from shame, deceit, and vanity as these are false emotions that are blocking your true heart. Enter the transformative space of true self-awareness and authenticity at Point Six, where you can cultivate your ability for authenticity and truthfulness, taught in the Enneagram as the Three's virtue. This is where you will reclaim your balance and the Grace and courage to be your authentic self.

Responses to Conflicts

Unhealthy Reaction

Vanity over authenticity; narcissism; false sense of self-image; inaction; jealousy; avoidance; emotional distortion; shame; misdirected anger; inability to speak up during true conflict or opportunities for personal growth; distorting the truth to fulfill a need to be seen as valuable; emotionally demonstrative displays aimed at people who challenge your identity of being a good/valuable/worthy/successful person

Healthy Reaction

Pause for honest reflection; courage; compassion; empathy; emotional honesty; externally focused; balanced self-awareness and communal awareness; outspoken and fierce challenges to things that don't affect your personal world; genuine desire to be present and honest with no hidden agenda; ability to take action; motivational charisma manifests and inspires others to do better and strive for success

Finding Your Place at Point Three

We asked individuals to describe their Enneagram journey to help illustrate how the energy is expressed at each of the Enneagram points. Point Three is represented by Marilyne's journey.

I discovered my type in the context of a coaching certification program where I was first introduced to the Enneagram. As soon as Type Three was described I identified with it immediately—the focus on achievement, the ability to become what others wanted me to be, and the belief that I was a superstar.

The initial discovery of my type primarily focused on what I saw as the positive aspects of Type Three with little recognition that I also possessed the less attractive aspect of the type.

I was happy to identify as a Three. In learning about each type, my comparative judgment kicked in and I quickly identified which types I thought were "good," and I was happy that I identified as a type that was more socially acceptable and desirable. I was in strong denial that I had any of the less attractive characteristics of the type and did not see how shame and inadequacy were a core part of my personality.

The Enneagram was one of the tools that helped me understand the deeper insecurity that drove me to constantly achieve. It has been a difficult journey to accept that my self-worth is inherent and not tied to what I do. Creating space for being, relaxation, and rest has been an important counterpoint to my workaholic tendencies and the need to appear successful.

Getting in touch with my heart's vulnerability has been both rewarding and challenging. My heart was extremely defended, and I feared intimacy. There was a deeply hidden belief that if I revealed my true self to another I would be judged and rejected. I believed that I was loved for what I did but not for who I am. Through the love of friends and family and through supportive environments I discovered that the more vulnerable I am, the more intimate and closer my relationships become. Being more authentically myself became the basis for more truthful, heartfelt, and real relationships.

As I became more authentic, I have moved away from exclusively focusing on other's needs as a way for people to like me and look up to me. I no longer believe that I must do everything myself. As a result, my relationships are now more reciprocal as I've learned to communicate my needs and accept help from others. In my determination to get things done, I would ignore my body. I suffer from chronic back pain and would regularly ignore the recurring pain in a drive to get things done. I am learning to tune in to my body's intelligence by slowing down and resting rather than pushing through.

The Enneagram has evolved from being a tool to better understand my personality to a roadmap on my spiritual path. I remain action-oriented and focused on doing but have an increasing capacity to catch myself when I am pushing to get something done rather than being in flow with reality.

My capacity to be in presence has increased. Presence has allowed me to show up in the world authentically *and with an open heart. I am less preoccupied with how people perceive me and the image I project. What is now meaningful to me is the ability to connect authentically with others responding to who they are and what arises in the moment rather than becoming the ideal I think they want to see.*

I am learning to let go of control and the belief that I am responsible for everything. Basic trust in the benevolence and harmony of the universe has allowed me to relax and accept reality as it arises even when it is challenging. I continue to explore my fear of being abandoned and rejected as well as the feeling of never being enough. I am gaining a better understanding of how these fears are behind my drive to achieve and always do more.

Most importantly I have learned to be with myself and not to suppress my emotions as they arise. I know that there is a space within me where love, peace, and joy reside and that they are always available to me. My need to seek love and acceptance outside myself has lessened as I touch into a universal love and unity with all things.

MARILYNE, UNITED STATES

REFLECTIONS FOR POINT THREE

* How do you resonate with the basic fear at Point Three?

* How does the basic desire at Point Three manifest for you?

* How do you resonate with the core wound at Point Three?

* Consider the energy at Point Three: What do you feel is missing from your being?

* What are you searching for?

* What does failure look like for you? How does it make you feel?

Point Four: *The Individualist*

4

Expressive, Dramatic, Self-absorbed, Temperamental

"I am good or okay if I am true to myself and to my feelings."

Basic Desire: To find self and true significance, to create an identity, to be unique and authentic

Basic Fear: To feel ordinary or lacking personal significance, to be inauthentic and mundane

Core Motivation: To express true self and unique individuality, to create and to be surrounded with beauty, to maintain certain moods and feelings, to withdraw and protect self-image, to take care of emotional needs before attending to anything else, to attract a "rescuer"

Core Wound: Self-suffering—disconnection from nurturing and protective figure: *"I must accept my uniqueness and suffering or else I will not be seen."*

TRADITIONAL ENNEAGRAM LANGUAGE

PASSION	FIXATION	VIRTUE
ENVY	MELANCHOLY	EQUANIMITY

TRANSITIONAL ENNEAGRAM LANGUAGE

Manifestation of Suffering in Our Shadow Side	Pattern of Behavior When Trapped by Personal Challenge	Releasing Ego Agenda & Stepping into Essence of Being
a toxic pattern of comparing struggles to the ease at which everyone else seems to exist, used to highlight or construct an outlet for emotional fulfillment	*a deep state of despair fueled by negative comparisons and fantasized reality of how sad and disappointing things have become*	*an acceptance of the absolute fluctuation of emotions and the balance of emotional honesty and connection to others*

Examples of Four Energy: Rumi, Sylvia Plath, Rihanna, Frida Kahlo, Edgar Allan Poe, Prince, Billie Eilish, Angelina Jolie, Anne Frank, Kat Von D., Jackie Kennedy Onassis, Joni Mitchell, Amy Winehouse, Meryl Streep, Marilyn Manson, Frédéric Chopin, Pyotr I. Tchaikovsky, Virginia Woolf, Anaïs Nin, Tennessee Williams, J.D. Salinger, Anne Rice, David Bowie, Billie Holiday, Judy Garland

Wings

Four has wing access to Point Three and Point Five

FOUR WITH A THREE WING

AUTHENTIC SELF	*SHADOW SELF*
motivated	*deeply narcissistic*
driven to stay authentic	*deceptive*
accomplished	*extremely image-conscious and insecure about self*
understand feelings and motivation of others	*detached from compassion and connection*

FOUR WITH A FIVE WING

AUTHENTIC SELF	*SHADOW SELF*
curious and problem-solving	*withdrawn and unfocused on real-world problems*
authentic to self	*egotistical*
without shame	*unable to live with social norms and within typical rules*
ability to remain objective and connected	
visionary	

*"At the end of the day, we can endure much
more than we think we can."*

FRIDA KAHLO

Lines & Arrows

Four has lines with arrows that connect to Point One and Point Two

FOUR TO ONE

AUTHENTIC SELF	SHADOW SELF
balanced and practical in living authentically	hypercritical of self and others
emotionally grounded	overly rigid
separate fantasy from reality	judgmental
	hold on to polarities

FOUR TO TWO

AUTHENTIC SELF	SHADOW SELF
ability to get out of internalized emotions	feeling of fakeness with compassion or inauthenticity
connect to others with authenticity and genuine empathy	counterbalance with overinflated ego-driven behaviors
connected to being supportive and helpful	

"I feel confident imposing change on myself. It's a lot more fun progressing than looking back. That's why I need to throw curve balls."

DAVID BOWIE

Summary

"Wisdom tells us we are not worthy; love tells us we are. My life flows between the two." These lines from the 13th-century Persian poet Rumi capture the complex nature of Four energy. If you stand at Point Four, the dichotomy of light and dark plays a major role in how you navigate life. You have a deep appreciation for finding beauty in an ugly world by honoring the depth of emotion and the complexities of life. As a Four, you may have felt like something was missing, even from early in your childhood, as if you were incomplete—and yet you continue to stay true to who you are. The search for your identity and how you project yourself to the outside world is rooted in the shame or guilt you feel about how you have or have not defined your own identity. The Four energy you live in can sometimes cause you to construct a fantasy world in which you play out different scenarios through your experiences. At times you become the person you think you want to be, and at other times you may spiral down into the pain and suffering you have experienced throughout your life. While usually authentic and true to yourself as a Four, you may sometimes find it difficult to deal with or acknowledge the reality of your own shame or guilt.

If the dominant energy you experience resides at Point Four, you may feel compelled to honor your authentic self and stay true to who you are and what you stand for. You may even describe your experience as a deep appreciation and awareness for the wide spectrum of human emotions, oftentimes aligning it to a transformation of pain and suffering. The gift of your energy at Point Four is a double-edged sword: understanding the broad spectrum of emotion and finding the light in the darkest moments while at the same time naturally gravitating toward and absorbing the darkness. This energy can sometimes transform into something creative, artistic, or aesthetically expressive. The metamorphosis of pain and suffering into something poetic, beautiful, transformative, or cathartic is a common theme among all Fours. The experience of being overly dramatic, moody, and emotional may not be uncommon for you at Point Four. You may even thrive on the fact that people consider you outside of "normal," thinking that being a unique human somehow gives you value. Deep down you just want to be accepted for who you are, but do you truly know your authentic self? The fantasies you have constructed to try to explain yourself do not actually define you. When you are operating within the healthy Levels of Development, you can begin to recognize that you are a whole human being capable of amazing things— just let go of the persistent search for something inside of you that you believe is missing. Whatever it is, it has always been there; you just need to unearth it.

Levels of Development

Healthy

As a Four in the healthy Levels of Development, you become kind and emotionally aware; you are balanced in your ability to hold space without falling into the pain. You have found equanimity in maintaining a balance of emotional intelligence and rational reasoning. The need to create the experience of a deep emotional state in order to maintain a false sense of identity fades away, and you are able to feel whole and connected to others. Being fully aware of the broad spectrum of human emotions and the highs and lows that are inherent in everyone makes you an expert in knowing how to behave, react, and offer support in whatever form is necessary during conflict. You become a seeker of beauty, and you want to share that beauty with everyone around you in an open, joyful, and inspirational way.

Average

Most humans reside within these average levels and fluctuate up or down depending on the circumstances they find themselves in. As you drop down into the average Levels of Development, the ego agenda begins to take over. The fluctuations can create opportunities for you to pause and cultivate the presence needed to examine your thoughts and actions and course correct. This allows you to move up in the levels and avoid falling back into unhealthy patterns of behavior and thought. However, as the ability for honest self-reflection and course correction wanes, shame, fear, and emotional distortion become the primary motivators that distort reality, resulting in a false narrative emerging and a flicker of disdain for other humans who seem to live with ease. This disconnect may trigger your resentment and envy, which masks your own unhealed wounds that you avoid truly acknowledging.

Some parts of you can see the path back to the light and happiness within you, but as a Four drops into the Levels of Development, the path back becomes hazy. Falling into a state of melancholy, you can become detached and emotionally distorted. You seek out outlets for your fantasies and the realities you have constructed to live out your pain and suffering. The feeling of overwhelm is not an uncommon experience for you in this space. It can feel like a riptide trying to carry you out, and at some point you decide to swim with the current to escape it. You often return to a state of despair over and over while you experience fleeting moments of hope and healing. You tend to hold on to your emotions, believing that this is the only thing that makes you who you are. In this space, you can develop an aversion to accepting reality and things as they are by becoming emotionally paralyzed, judgmental, self-indulgent, depressed, and apathetic. The guilt and shame at these levels can morph into a combination of overwhelm and melancholy and cause you to drop further down the levels. You can use these moments of reflection as a wake-up call to step into a healthy space or allow them to deteriorate into a toxic pattern of thoughts and behaviors. It takes a great deal of self-reflection and inner work to rise through the levels and avoid dropping further.

Unhealthy

As you drop into the unhealthy levels, you become deeply narcissistic and self-absorbed, creating a unique persona that you believe makes you better than "ordinary" people. Deep shame, despair, and overall emotional manipulation are the primary motivators that distort your reality, resulting in a disdain for other humans who seem to live with ease. This disconnect may trigger your deep resentment and envy, which prevents you from not only dealing with but even acknowledging your own unhealed wounds. You absorb experiences and distort your reality to victimize yourself, believing that your pain and suffering are all that you are; you begin to think that you have nothing else if you do not hold on to these feelings. Your narcissism and internal fantasy world leave you little room to find compassion or empathy for other people, which leads you down a path of selfish, destructive, and deeply unhealthy behaviors.

Instincts

Self-Preservation Four

If you are a Self-Preservation Four, you may be more introverted or internally focused than the other Instincts in Four. You focus your energy on cultivating an environment that showcases your appreciation for beauty and creativity. Much like One energy, you are very particular about your environment and the general atmosphere you create for yourself. Unlike One energy, you will allow your emotions to swing like a pendulum and use the highs and lows to dictate your behaviors, actions, and the elements within your life that you feel are important. You enjoy the extremes of emotion and make the most of both the good and the bad; this applies not only to yourself but to the people around you. You will stand with your friends during painful times and joyous times when others tend to back away or feel uncomfortable. The Self-Preservation instinct in Four might make you resemble Seven energy at times, as you focus much of your attention on your own needs and like to live life fully and without restraint. You might have a hard time connecting with others you deem unworthy, boring, too reserved, or lacking in taste, as deep down you are trying to manage your own shame around your self-identification. The Self-Preservation instinct in Four can create some challenges when connecting with others but can also create a person who is deeply connected to the wide spectrum of human emotion with a deep appreciation for beauty in diversity—people, experiences, cultures, hobbies, traditions, and so on.

Social Four

As a Social Four you tend to be concerned with your individual uniqueness and focus your energy on how unlike you are to everyone else; this is your gift and your burden. You are more socially motivated than the other Instincts in Four, but often feel as though you don't fit in and can't relate to others. Much like the Social Three energy, you can spend a considerable amount of energy comparing yourself to others and long to be a part of the top social groups, but you feel as if you will always fall short. You may manifest an exotic or eccentric persona to compensate for your lack of confidence in fitting into social situations, but you still long to be accepted with no strings attached. It's likely that you still need assurance that you are accepted and welcomed into group settings and must overcome the constant battle between being defined by your "outsider" mentality and feeling like it is your disadvantage. However, the Social instinct in Four can create a truly unique person who adds a new perspective to any group setting, as long as you are willing to let go of your internalized fantasies and feelings of inadequacy and step into your authentic self with Grace and emotional honesty.

Sexual Four

If you identify with the Sexual instinct in Four, you may focus your energy on finding and holding on to a "rescuer" or a person who understands and appreciates you. This is a common theme for all Instincts in Four, but the Sexual instinct is the embodiment of the intense romanticism associated with Four energy. Much like Sexual Threes and Twos, you enjoy being admired and will strive to be alluring and irresistible, oftentimes allowing your emotions to swing wildly back and forth from love to hate as a way of making yourself feel more mysterious or intriguing. You want to be desired, and you want other people to acknowledge that you are desirable, but you often harbor deep doubt around your own desirability—similar to Two energy. Envy is most clearly expressed in this instinct, as you romanticize your relationships with others, and then resent them for being as desirable as you wish you were yourself. While radiating a magnetic energy that draws people in, you can also repel people when you feel slighted by the lack of reciprocated attention. The Sexual instinct in Four makes for an intensity that many can find overwhelming, but more often than not people will gravitate toward this energy without knowing it. As a Sexual Four you can add a deeper level of intimacy and connection to any relationship, as long as you remain balanced and honest with your emotional needs.

Challenges and Overcoming the Egoic Agenda

While radiating an energy of a unique and special individual, your inner narrative has created self-doubt and a feeling that something is fundamentally missing in you. The deep fear of being ordinary may cause you to compare your life to other people, particularly the severity of your suffering or the lack of ease with which you live. This can send you into a downward spiral where your internal narrative keeps you trapped in an envious, toxic, and contrived fantasy.

Your gaze is often drawn to honoring the emotional intelligence and complex balance within any given situation. While there is a deep connection to emotional responses, the ever-present challenge is maintaining an intentional awareness of emotional honesty without dropping into a state of unhealthy emotional fatigue or destructive fantasies. A common experience among Four energy is the construction of an alternate reality where emotions and feelings can be played out and cause the subsequent entrapment of emotional distortion to fulfill some hidden fantasy. While you do have the capacity for an enormous amount of healing and truly beautiful energy, the challenge is knowing when you are falling into unhealthy internalization of emotion instead of engaging in emotional honesty with yourself and other humans.

You can see and hold space for the
beauty in the wounded and broken.

This is a rare and precious gift.

The Path of Inner Work

The Four's personal challenge, or passion of envy as it is called in the Enneagram, is a toxic pattern of comparing your struggles to the ease at which everyone else seems to exist. Your Four energy feels incomplete or lacking in some way and seeks ways to point it out to yourself and live within your own melodramatic despair. The intensity that your Four energy brings into everything matters and drives you to create distortions of reality in which you can live out your fears and pain while you try to figure it out. This conscripted stance is the default to live in your emotions rather than act on them. Your unique way of navigating challenges can lead you to a dark downward spiral of despair, a concept that is taught as the fixation of melancholy. This is where you get trapped and your shame and low self-worth become the guidance for your automatic pilot. The internalization and rejection/ transformation of your shame is your way of masking your Achilles' heel: being ordinary. The invitation to move into a healthy space is attainable when you access the gift of emotional honesty, compassion, and focused balance at Point Two, moving away from narcissism, envy, and melancholy, as these are toxic emotions that are blocking your true heart. Enter the transformative space at Point One in the Body Center, where you can establish your equanimity, taught in the Enneagram as the Four's virtue. This is where you will reclaim your balance, presence, and ability to honor your authentic self with Grace and self-confidence.

Responses to Conflicts

Unhealthy Reaction

Judgmental thinking; depressive spiraling; isolation; emotional distortion; dual reality; despair; hypersensitivity to accusations; alienation of other people; blaming everyone but yourself and then pushing others away; delusion that you are wholly unique and do not need to act within socially acceptable "limits;" envious ways of thinking and behaving; live in your emotions and feel that your own suffering is more than you can bear, so the thought of dealing with other people's suffering is unimaginable; truly depressed and lost at the sheer volume of suffering in the world you become detached; fearing the overwhelm of sadness and pain you will lash out and perpetually push people away and hold onto the deep and paralyzing emotional torment

Healthy Reaction

Genuine empathy; equanimity; hope; kindness; intentional pause for reflection; highly creative and deeply intuitive; inspired; emotionally connected; profound and insightful; you maintain a safe space for people to express their emotions with the reassurance that someone is genuinely listening with an empathetic heart; a distinguishing characteristic unlike any other type, ability to transform all experiences—both positive and negative—into opportunities for growth and reflection, strong connection to your own humanity, which gives you a heightened ability to understand others' feelings and emotions as both valuable and appropriate, balanced approach to life through light and dark

Finding Your Place at Point Four

We asked individuals to describe their Enneagram journey to help illustrate how the energy is expressed at each of the Enneagram points. Point Four is represented by Sterling's journey.

My brother took an Enneagram class at an Orange County community college in 1995, taught by Robert Olson, Ph.D., and then read his book Stepping Out Within. *He called me up one day and said, "I'm taking a personality class, and I'm a Four and you're a Three." After hearing the Type Four description, I knew we were the same type, but he was picking up on my Three wing.*

I dove deeper into the Enneagram and started doing my own research. I finally understood why I felt more sensitive and self-conscious than everyone I grew up with, in a success-driven, conservative suburb. I had

always felt like something was wrong with me, and the Type Four description gave me an understanding of the shame and insignificance that characterizes the type. Honestly I also felt a little bit vindicated after feeling so worthless and rejected for so long.

When I discovered my type and began identifying my behaviors, I used it as a way to defend myself from being hurt again. Instead of being rejected, I used the Enneagram as a way to find my tribe and the people who I thought would understand me. Not surprisingly, this never really worked the way I wanted it to, and I still felt alone. The Enneagram teachings really became clear to me once I started studying Tibetan Buddhism and developed a meditation practice. There I realized that the only way to soften the personality was to develop kindness toward myself. This realization is where I made a shift and realized the true purpose of the Enneagram.

Today, I continue to work with my harsh inner critic to allow me to soften toward myself and other people. I try to remember that the Type Four personality structure has helped me survive and try to have a sense of humor around continuing old patterns, often using self-observation and kindness to notice when I'm on autopilot. Also, since Type Four has a disconnection with the body, I'm starting to play around with having faith in its intelligence. Working with the Instincts has become important work, where I can see the missing parts of my life come together when focusing on the social instinct. I continue to seek out community on the path so that I'm not doing the work alone and can learn from all of the types.

STERLING, CALIFORNIA

REFLECTIONS FOR POINT FOUR

❖ How do you resonate with the basic fear at Point Four?

❖ How does the basic desire at Point Four manifest for you?

❖ How do you resonate with the core wound at Point Four?

❖ Consider the energy at Point Four: What do you feel is missing from your being?

❖ What are you searching for?

❖ What does it look like when you feel misunderstood, out of place, or unseen?

Chapter 5

The Head Center

5-6-7

The Head Center, or Thinking Triad, is the center where Points Five, Six, and Seven reside. These three energies have a wisdom that comes from internalization and reflection. As conscious human beings, we all possess the ability to internalize and process information to find solutions; however, for the Five, Six, and Seven this energy is at the core of their actions, behaviors, and beliefs. This group is centered around inner guidance—a persistent state of getting stuck in their head—and expressing or managing their fear in different ways.

The capacity for honest reflection and finding perspective during times of conflict without reacting impulsively, instinctually, or emotionally resides within the Head Center. They are the points that can see the big picture and access a multiperspective balance, because they are wired to make space for reflection and intentional presence more readily than most.

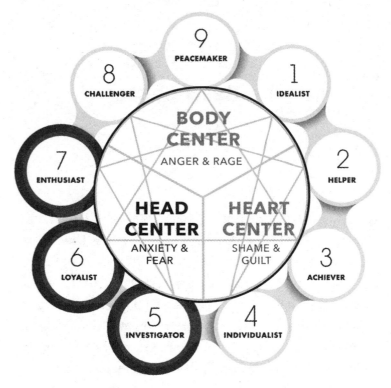

The Head Center of the Enneagram

The Wall of Fear and Anxiety

People who identify with the Head Center points have a distinct experience with the emotion of fear or anxiety, more so than the other centers. All humans experience fear, as it is a basic human emotion; however, for the

Head Center fear is the catalyst behind many of their patterns of behavior. During times of pain and suffering, either internally or externally, Head types experience an uncomfortable cognitive dissonance that often transforms into internalized anxiety and redirected fear. This pattern consequently connects Fives, Sixes, and Sevens to the capacity for reflection and guided intention. The Head Center is concerned with looking to the future as a way of finding solutions, support, and guidance to manage their fears. The management of fear and anxiety is dependent on how the point in question is attempting to reassure themselves, fulfill the core motivation, and avoid the basic fear.

Many people within the Head Center experience a paralyzing wall of fear and anxiety surrounding a particular unhealed or unexplored internal wound. This wall creates a barrier to accessing the authentic self and the method in which it is addressed or ignored is dependent on the individual. For some Head types, the fear can stem from an early memory of feeling insecure, unsafe, unsupported, unfulfilled, or alone. Each point deals with their fear differently, but when we are stuck in a toxic pattern of behavior, the fear we feel internally is often transformed into an outward expression aimed at redirecting our fears onto others in one way or another.

For Fives, the fear is often channeled into cultivating space for security and psychological safety. Their fear of being depleted of their resources propels them into isolating themselves from whatever is causing their fear.

For Sixes, the fear is ever-present and typically infiltrates every aspect of their behaviors and beliefs. They internalize the fear and then project it outward as a shield from anything that may affect them, which in turn reignites the fear from within.

For Sevens, the fear is not usually outwardly recognized as fear, but rather a warning system to avoid fear. Sevens are unique in that their deep internal fears and anxiety are expertly hidden by their typically adventurous and spontaneous nature. Fear is not an emotion many Sevens are willing to admit or deal with, so they redirect their attention to avoid what may be the underlying cause of their anxiety.

We will explore this concept in depth for each point later on in the book, but the main takeaway is that in the Head Center the anxiety and fear can be masking a much deeper issue.

Point Five: *The Investigator*

5

Perceptive, Innovative, Secretive, Isolated

"I am good or okay if I know and have mastered something."

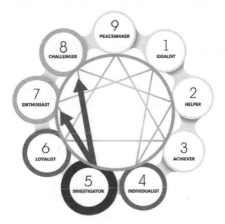

Basic Desire: To be capable and competent, to have knowledge and wisdom

Basic Fear: To feel useless, helpless, incapable, and incompetent, to be depleted of resources

Core Motivation: To possess knowledge, to understand the environment, to have everything figured out as a way of defending the self from threats from the environment, to be able to retreat inward and collect more resources (wisdom, knowledge, time, answers, information, etc.)

Core Wound: Self-isolation—disconnection from nurturing and protective figure: *"I must withdraw and develop my own mastery or I will not belong or survive."*

TRADITIONAL ENNEAGRAM LANGUAGE

PASSION	FIXATION	VIRTUE
AVARICE	STINGINESS	NON-ATTACHMENT

⬇ ⬇ ⬇

TRANSITIONAL ENNEAGRAM LANGUAGE

Manifestation of Suffering in Our Shadow Side	Pattern of Behavior When Trapped by Personal Challenge	Releasing Ego Agenda & Stepping into Essence of Being
a relentless search for more resources and more knowledge in order to calm inner fears of feeling useless and incapable	*an unquenchable need to hoard resources, gathering time, knowledge, energy, and material possessions to feel secure*	*detach from the need to think everything through in order to protect self and resources, find security in fair and objective perspective of acquiring, transforming, and sharing wisdom and resources*

Examples of Five Energy: Buddha, Albert Einstein, Eckhart Tolle, Friedrich Nietzsche, Jane Goodall, Stephen Hawking, Stanley Kubrick, Ted Kaczynski, Anita Hill, Vincent van Gogh, Bill Gates, Mark Zuckerberg, John Walker Lindh, Timothy McVeigh, Phil Spector, Edvard Munch, Georgia O'Keeffe, Salvador Dali, Emily Dickinson, Agatha Christie, James Joyce, Stephen King

Wings

Five has wing access to Point Four and Point Six

FIVE WITH A FOUR WING

AUTHENTIC SELF	SHADOW SELF
creative problem solving	deeply withdrawn
balanced perspective	overly sensitive
deep focus and attentiveness	egotistical and self-centered
ability to find the connections when others cannot	detached from compassion and connection to others

FIVE WITH A SIX WING

AUTHENTIC SELF	SHADOW SELF
focused and calm during conflict	deeply insecure and anxious
passion for learning and finding solutions to collective issues	cold and aloof
ability to connect the dots	struggle to relate or connect with others

"Thousands of candles can be lighted from a single candle, and the life of the candle will not be shortened. Happiness never decreases by being shared."

BUDDHA

Lines & Arrows

Five has lines with arrows that connect to Point Eight and Point Seven

FIVE TO EIGHT

AUTHENTIC SELF	SHADOW SELF
find power and forcefulness to speak up assertive with confidence and clarity ability to take action	incredibly stubborn and harsh intellectually arrogant outwardly dismissive of others cold and unfeeling

FIVE TO SEVEN

AUTHENTIC SELF	SHADOW SELF
open-minded and optimistic able to see value in others and connect to share wisdom ability to remain present instead of withdrawing	scattered and distractible detached from others disconnected from finding common ground harsh and condescending

"Whatever we believe about how we got to be the extraordinary creatures we are today is far less important than bringing our intellect to bear on how do we get together now around the world and get out of the mess that we've made."

JANE GOODALL

Summary

In the early 1900s, a Lebanese American writer and philosopher named Khalil Gibran said "Knowledge of the self is the mother of all knowledge. So it is incumbent on me to know my self, to know it completely, to know its minutiae, its characteristics, its subtleties, and its very atoms." Though he went on to write *The Prophet*, *The Madman*, and *Broken Wings*, three globally recognized books, he rejected the moniker of "philosopher," and considered himself instead a visual artist, writer, and poet who valued his privacy and rejected fame. Khalil Gibran was the epitome of an Enneagram Five; he was wise and knowledgeable in many different areas, he actively sought out answers to life's big questions, and he rejected mainstream avenues and titles. If you stand at Point Five, then the pursuit of knowledge is more than likely the catalyst for many of the things you do. As a Five, you have an innate drive to make sense of chaos and to seek out ways to feel more capable and competent. You seek out answers and strive to acquire more knowledge as a way of protecting yourself and planning ahead for the future. There is a great deal of anxiety behind your pursuit of information, and the reason behind the anxiety can often be traced back to your insecurity around your own well-being and how you have managed to cope with your fears. You are concerned with planning for the future and calming your fears by hoarding your resources, almost as if they will form a security blanket around you.

If Point Five is where you stand on the Enneagram map, you are likely a truly knowledgeable, wise, and capable person. You may place a great deal of importance on your capability and the need to maintain your resources—time, knowledge, personal space, tools, and so on—and oftentimes view others as unworthy of an invitation into your hoard of resources. The experience of being misunderstood or of being underestimated in your wisdom and capability may be a common experience for you at Point Five. You deny people the opportunity to connect with you out of fear and insecurity, and in turn, you deprive yourself of true wisdom and opportunities for growth and compassion. An intentional shift to find presence and connection will allow you to grow as a true visionary. On the other side, your natural predisposition toward finding order in the chaos makes you a truly valuable friend and skillful architect in other people's lives. When you are operating within healthy Levels of Development, you become more willing to let people in and connect with them to find solutions and create support structures for long-term friendships and partnerships. You seem to be able to remain objective and impartial, even during deep disconnects, and search for the road back to reconnection with wisdom and innovative vision. This makes you a trustworthy teller of truth and a dependable and wise friend for many different types of people.

Levels of Development

Healthy

When you are operating in the healthy Levels of Development, you become secure in your ability to connect with others without the fear of feeling overwhelmed or depleted. You are willing to connect to others in the hope of finding subject matter experts in whatever space you find yourself in. You become a leader who establishes credibility and sustainability for whatever cause or movement you are fighting for, oftentimes "behind the scenes" or in fundamental positions of power. You are a true expert and a keeper of truth in whatever area you are passionate about; you can cut through the falsities of any argument with precision and strength. You become a keeper of the historical path that allows us to put the pieces of history back together. Oftentimes you can become the institutional source of wisdom and narrative of your community.

Average

Most humans reside within these average levels and fluctuate up or down depending on the circumstances they find themselves in. As you drop down into the average Levels of Development, the ego agenda begins to take over. The fluctuations can create opportunities for you to pause and cultivate the presence needed to examine your thoughts and actions and course correct. This allows you to move up in the levels and avoid falling back into unhealthy patterns of behavior and thought. However, as the ability for honest self-reflection and course correction wanes, you can become emotionally stunted and get stuck in your head trying to make sense of things. In between fleeting moments of reconnecting the dots and seeing the path back to your authentic self, you begin to allow your fear to creep in. The desire to disconnect and withdraw inward is caused by overwhelming moments of hopelessness and fear. You may seek out ways to avoid connection and believe you must hold on to your resources to survive, whether it is time, knowledge, groups, books, or anything that you may have acquired.

In this space you become unwilling to connect and your stubbornness can come off as intellectual arrogance. The thought of the connection to others is exhausting, so you withdraw and isolate yourself out of fear of becoming depleted and thus rendered incapacitated or underprepared. You may have flickers of connectedness and see the value in sharing your wisdom, but the fear of becoming depleted or overwhelmed can quickly shift you into self-isolation. You may offer bullet points to a solution, but you intentionally withhold the full picture, just in case. The fear and anxiety at these levels can morph into a combination of overwhelm and detachment and cause you to drop further down the levels. You can use these moments of reflection as a wake-up call to step into a healthy space or allow them to deteriorate into a toxic pattern of thoughts and behaviors. It takes a great deal of self-reflection and inner work to rise through the levels and avoid dropping further.

Unhealthy

As you drop into the unhealthy levels you can become highly unstable, obsessive, isolated, arrogant, detached, and egotistical. You start to justify your destructive actions and toxic beliefs from the unhealthy energy of Point Five. You can use your vast knowledge for ill gain, sometimes out of spite or misdirected fear. Anxiety, greed, fear, and insecurity are the primary motivators that distort your reality resulting in disdain for anyone or anything that may compromise your existence or threaten your hoard of resources. You may become a deeply detached and extremist individual who isolates and submerges yourself in whatever resources you have collected to sustain your biased or delusional perspectives. You are incredibly arrogant and narcissistic in your behaviors aimed at belittling people; deep down you are trying to cover the reality that you are a bundle of fear and anxiety.

Instincts

Self-Preservation Five

If you identify as a Self-Preservation Five, you are likely even more introverted or internally focused than the other Instincts in Five. You focus your energy on cultivating an environment that allows you to easily retreat inward with little connection to the outside world. Oftentimes you will reduce your footprint on the world; this is true in both space, relationships, needs, and external dependencies. As a Self-Pres Five you are probably content by yourself with your hobbies and interests, and have little patience for anyone or anything that may overwhelm you or drain you of your energy and resources. You enjoy being independent and actively resist situations that may cause you to rely on others for anything. You may have a very hard time connecting with others you find intrusive or emotionally demanding, as deep down you are trying to manage your own fear of feeling depleted or overwhelmed. The Self-Preservation instinct in Five can create some serious challenges when connecting with others but can also enable you to be unexpectedly warm, affectionate, and generous when people respect and honor your need for space and privacy.

Social Five

As a Social Five you tend to be slightly more extroverted than the other Instincts in Five, as you enjoy finding a niche you can carve out in your social group. You enjoy being seen as the quintessential source of wisdom or advice that your close inner circle can come to with questions. While you may be more socially motivated than the other Instincts in Five, you still need space to recharge and find peace much like Nine energy. You can have a hard time relating to others when the discussion veers from your area of expertise or when you lose interest in whatever may be happening at that particular moment. Much like Eight energy, in terms of power and control, you use your knowledge and wisdom to wield your power and exert control over others, sometimes with an air of arrogance. This can present a challenge when you drop into unhealthy Levels of Development and become callous and cold. However, when healthy you can establish long-lasting bonds with many different types of people and elevate the level of shared knowledge, depth of conversation, and inquisitive endeavors of any social group.

Sexual Five

If you are a Sexual Five you may live with the constant battle between wanting to find a deep connection and the natural instinct of a Five's need for independence. This is a common theme for most Fives, as being human makes us all desire some sort of connection, but the Sexual instinct in Five creates a deep desire to find connection with another person all while battling the insecurity surrounding your social skills. Much like Seven energy, you tend to be more talkative and personable than the other Instincts in Five, but you can quickly retreat inward when things become overwhelming or you allow your anxieties to surface. When the Sexual instinct and the natural wisdom inherent in Five energy combine, you can resemble a Four in your ability to tap into your vivid imagination and create incredibly complex realities that you can play out to attract a partner or deep relationships with others. As a Sexual Five you can add a deeper level of intimacy, imagination, and connection to any relationship, as long as you find the ability to stay present and tap into your natural ability to communicate with people.

Challenges and Overcoming the Egoic Agenda

At Point Five, you may exude confidence in your wisdom and ability to figure things out, but deep down you are hiding the constant worry of being incapacitated by external influences. You may struggle to maintain the balance of knowing enough about something and knowing too much. You lose focus on what's important and allow your fear and anxiety to push you inward where you withdraw and isolate yourself from others. The deep fear of being incapable or underprepared, often aligned with the anxiety around being depleted of resources, can cause you to hoard your knowledge and resources and retreat inward.

As a Five, you are the vault keeper of a broad spectrum of knowledge, expertise, and valuable resources. However, you probably have an aversion to readily sharing your wisdom or resources with others, or of being seen as valuable only for what you know. You may seek out ways to avoid connection and believe you must hold on to your resources to survive, whether it is time, knowledge, groups, books, or anything that you may have acquired. In this space, you become unwilling to connect, stubborn and intellectually arrogant, cold and angry, fearful and apathetic. The innovative thought processes, internalization, isolation of self, and a strong drive to figure things out create the comfort zone for you at Point Five. However, the polarity here is managing the need for more information and resources in order to prevent yourself from feeling incapable or overwhelmed while not hoarding or taking on so much to the point of retreating into yourself, feeling depleted, and becoming a withdrawn recluse. Your energy seeks out a way to calm your fears by constantly looking for answers while at the same time detaching yourself from those around you.

Your search for knowledge has no worth if you are unwilling to share it freely with others.

The Path of Inner Work

The Five's personal challenge, or passion of avarice as it is called in the Enneagram, is a deep desire to locate and acquire any and all resources that will ensure you are knowledgeable, competent, and prepared. Your Five energy seeks more knowledge, more books, more sources, more answers, more of everything. The intensity that your Five energy brings into everything matters and fuels your fear of losing what resources you have collected, which may render you incapable of functioning. This conscripted stance is the default to justify your thirst to acquire more and retreat inward. Your unique way of navigating challenges can lead you to an unwillingness to share your knowledge and resources or to connect with other humans, a concept that is taught as the fixation of stinginess. This is where you get trapped and your fear and anxiety become the guidance for your automatic pilot. The hoarding and isolation you allow is your way of masking your Achilles' heel: fear. The invitation to move into a healthy space is attainable when you access the gift of freedom and balance at Point Seven, moving away from fear, avarice, and stinginess as these are toxic emotions that are blocking your true heart. Enter a transformative space at Point Eight where you can reclaim your strength and courage to take your wisdom out into the world, taught in the Enneagram as the Five's virtue of nonattachment.

This is where you will find your balance and connectivity to the world around you.

Responses to Conflicts

Unhealthy Reaction

Isolation; feeling depleted; detachment; intellectual arrogance; egotistical antagonism; denial; inability to access compassion; withdrawal; seclusion; overcompensation; antagonistic approach to opposing views; extreme/radical stance; argumentative and cynical; challenging accepted ways of behaving "just because you can;" being seen as only "valuable for what you know" and then lashing out at others for being undervalued; unwillingness to share knowledge and resources or to connect with other humans

Healthy Reaction

Connection to others; insight into creating systematic connection; gifting of knowledge; objective reasoning and ability to find a multiperspective approach; reflection on the big picture in order to connect the dots and find solutions for connecting across differences; instinct and decision making free from emotional distortions; the clear ability to gather information and create organized systems for change and progress; value diversity as a tool for acquiring more knowledge and perspective; freedom from destructive inner monologue and internalized fears

Finding Your Place at Point Five

We asked individuals to describe their Enneagram journey to help illustrate how the energy is expressed at each of the Enneagram points. Point Five is represented by Carolyn's journey.

I was introduced to Deborah Egerton by a mutual friend. We enjoyed one another's company, and I began to look forward to her trips to St. Croix. I didn't understand exactly what she did, but as a Five, I now understand why I was definitely intrigued. She seemed to know things about me, and I didn't know how this was possible. I had not known her long enough or shared very much personal information.

Deborah gave me my first Enneagram book, and I couldn't believe what I was reading. Initially I was confused. Could this be real? Eventually I was relieved and then amazed at how much it explained about my thoughts and feelings that I had not ever been able to express. I realized that I wanted to "do the work" because I knew this would yield great rewards. In the early days of learning the Enneagram I was spending so much time in my head, which created anxiety. But I was on the journey.

Deborah brought the Enneagram to St. Croix, and we worked together planning retreats for women.

I am a dermatologist, so my participation was to teach wellness while Deborah guided us through the energies of the Enneagram. As I continued this work I became much more intentionally introspective about my thoughts, feelings, reactions, and responses. I have an increased awareness of my presence. I am aware of when I am "in my head," and I know how important consistency is for me in my daily spiritual practices.

I review my daily Enneagram messages. I'm constantly learning and always wanting to grow to be the best I can be. What I know now is the best that I can be is just to be me. Letting love in has been a major growth step for me. When I celebrated a milestone birthday I danced as if no one was watching (I was on stage and everyone was watching!) I looked down and saw Deborah smiling at me. She knew this Five was finally free.

CAROLYN, ST. CROIX

REFLECTIONS FOR POINT FIVE

❖ How do you resonate with the basic fear at Point Five?

❖ How does the basic desire at Point Five manifest for you?

❖ How do you resonate with the core wound at Point Five?

❖ Consider the energy at Point Five: What do you feel is missing from your being?

❖ What are you searching for?

❖ What does it look like when you feel overwhelmed, depleted, or anxious?

Point Six: The Loyalist

Engaging, Responsible, Anxious, Suspicious

"I am good or okay if I am responsible and I do what is expected of me."

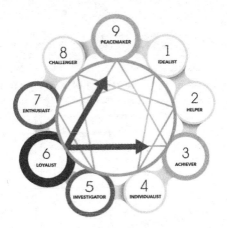

Basic Desire: To have security and stability, to have support and guidance

Basic Fear: To feel unstable or without guidance, to be without support

Core Motivation: To have security and backup plans, to feel supported by others, to have certitude and reassurance, to test the attitudes of others toward them, to fight against anxiety and insecurity

Core Wound: Self-doubt—attachment to the protective figure: *"I must find an authoritative voice to keep me safe or the worst-case scenario of my thinking will consume me."*

TRADITIONAL ENNEAGRAM LANGUAGE

PASSION	FIXATION	VIRTUE
FEAR	COWARDICE	COURAGE

TRANSITIONAL ENNEAGRAM LANGUAGE

Manifestation of Suffering in Our Shadow Side	Pattern of Behavior When Trapped by Personal Challenge	Releasing Ego Agenda & Stepping into Essence of Being
uncertainty and a deep distrust in all things: self, people, information, systems, authority, actions, beliefs, and behaviors	*a paralyzing pattern of panic, distrust, inaction, and helplessness when faced with challenges to stability and security*	*an acceptance of trust in self and others allows for purpose and strength in all things*

Examples of Six Energy: Richard Nixon, Sigmund Freud, Robert F. Kennedy, Malcolm X, George H.W. Bush, J.R.R. Tolkien, Michael Moore, Jimmy Kimmel, Prince Harry, Bono, Spike Lee, J. Edgar Hoover, Mindy Kaling, Rush Limbaugh, Ellen DeGeneres, Lewis Black, Chris Rock, Larry David, Tom Hanks, Mel Gibson, John Grisham, Mike Tyson, Bruce Springsteen, Woody Allen

Wings

Six has wing access to Point Five and Point Seven

SIX WITH A FIVE WING

AUTHENTIC SELF	SHADOW SELF
practical problem solving	incredibly pessimistic and cynical
passion for finding truth and fighting unfair systems	emotionally stunted
inner drive to be a part of something bigger than self	detached, cold, and aloof
	socially awkward and insensitive
	reactive and aggressive

SIX WITH A SEVEN WING

AUTHENTIC SELF	SHADOW SELF
dedicated to a cause	doubt in all things
deeply connected to the well-being of others	selfish and insensitive
loyal and optimistic	indecisive and scattered
engaged and sociable	focused on negative

"There is no fear when you choose love. The more you choose love, the more love is in your life. It gets easier and easier."

MELISSA ETHERIDGE

Lines & Arrows

Six has lines with arrows that connect to
Point Three and Point Nine

SIX TO THREE

AUTHENTIC SELF	SHADOW SELF
confidence and trust in self decisive action	narrow focus creates an isolated perspective
courageous and communicative	self-centered behaviors to gain leverage or security
outgoing and affable	overwhelm and exhaustion

SIX TO NINE

AUTHENTIC SELF	SHADOW SELF
balanced perspective	maintain status quo
driven to find collective peace and harmony	disregard for others
courageous action	incredibly detached
	apathetic
	distrusting

"In oneself lies the whole world and if you know how to look and learn, the door is there and the key is in your hand. Nobody on earth can give you either the key or the door to open, except yourself."

JIDDU KRISHNAMURTI

Summary

Steve Jobs once said, "Your time is limited, so don't waste it living someone else's life. Don't be trapped by dogma—which is living with the results of other people's thinking. Don't let the noise of others' opinions drown out your own inner voice. And most importantly, have the courage to follow your heart and intuition." These words should be repeated to Enneagram Sixes over and over and over again. If you stand at Point Six, you likely have a complicated relationship with your fear and your courage. As a Six, you have developed an internal committee in your head, constantly scanning for threats and establishing a plan for all scenarios. The incessant chatter of your mind is your way of working through your anxiety. You seek out solutions to assess potential threats to your safety, stability, and security, which is your complicated way of calming your fears and anxiety. You are likely concerned with the future and actively resist things or people that may threaten your plans for securing a stable foundation. There is an immense deal of insecurity and hesitancy behind almost everything you do, and the reason behind the anxiety can often be traced back to a lack of self-confidence and apprehension in trusting yourself and, in turn, trusting others.

If the dominant energy you experience is at Point Six, you may feel compelled by a need for security, stability, and support in all things. Loyalty, commitment, and the incessant internal chatter of a worrying mind create the comfort zone while the appearance of problems without clear solutions creates anxiety and frustration for you as a loyal, steadfast, dutiful individual that stands at Point Six. There is always something to be prepared for in today's world, and you take that responsibility to a molecular level; backup plans for the backup plans, preparing for worst-case scenarios, consulting the committee in your head before even considering taking action. The experience of being seen as scattered, fearful, indecisive, and cynical may not feel uncommon for you at Point Six. Your inner narrative may prevent you from connecting to other people and deprive you of the opportunity to find actual stability and guidance. On the other side, you have the capacity to become a valiant seeker of truth and connection when you allow your courage to manifest instead of keeping it hidden under your fear and anxiety. When you are operating within the healthy Levels of Development you become more trusting and develop the courage it takes to step out of your comfort zone and connect with people. This makes you a trustworthy teller of truth and a loyal friend to many different types of people.

Levels of Development

Healthy

When operating within the healthy Levels of Development, you can honor the value in truth and duty and stand up to destructive forces. You may challenge the systems designed to create disparities and inequities all while managing the polarity of fear and integrity. Your courageous spirit and the true force of your inner strength begin to guide you on your journey of becoming a leader in the fight for collective security. The anxiety and fear that once paralyzed you now evolve and make space for a decisive and truth-seeking champion who recognizes your fear as a wake-up call to take action. You will stand up and fight against any challenge to the stability and security of any human or group; cutting through the false narratives and the negativity with courage and compassion.

Average

Most humans reside within these average levels and fluctuate up or down depending on the circumstances they find themselves in. As you drop down into the average Levels of Development, the ego agenda begins to take over. The fluctuations can create opportunities for you to pause and cultivate the presence needed to examine your thoughts and actions and course correct. This allows you to move back up in the levels and avoid falling back into unhealthy patterns of behavior and thought. However, as the ability for honest self-reflection and course correction wanes, you can become suspicious of others and your own beliefs. You become reactive and unpredictable, focusing on the threats to your own security. You begin to allow the fear to creep in a little further. You can become fearful of change and uncertainty and struggle to acknowledge opportunities for growth and goodness to flourish. You may turn critical, panicky, passive-aggressive and sarcastic. Amid fleeting moments of clarity and focus, you are able to see a path back to your authentic self and the courage you have inside of you, but the path can become murky as you begin to question your own judgment and decisions.

In the average levels you are likely a wounded individual attempting to conceal your true fears by lashing out with distrustful and irrational beliefs and negativity aimed at anyone who threatens your perception of stability and security. Despite having the innate ability to see the big picture and access all perspectives in question, you often choose to select whatever data supports you in your quest to justify your own fear. Trust becomes a primary challenge as you drop lower into the Levels of Development. The fear and anxiety at these levels can morph into a combination of uncertainty, distrust, and suspicion which can cause you to drop further down the levels. You can use these moments of reflection as a wake-up call to step into a healthy space or allow them to deteriorate into a toxic pattern of thoughts and behaviors. It takes a great deal of self-reflection and inner work to rise through the levels and avoid dropping further.

Unhealthy

As you drop into the unhealthy levels, you can become incredibly unstable, nihilistic, irrationally belligerent, and self-destructive. You begin to justify your actions and beliefs from the unhealthy energy of Point Six. Fear, distrust, and paranoia are the primary motivators that distort your reality, resulting in disdain for humans who may be perceived as a threat or challenge to your way of life. As an unhealthy Six, you are likely to hold on to an unquestioned loyalty in favor of unfair and biased systems already in place out of fear of being left on uncertain or shaky ground. As you drop lower and lower into the levels, you become deeply distrustful of others but also of yourself; you are stuck in a destructive pattern of indecision and suspicion. Fearful, unstable, delusional, and unquestioningly loyal, you may cause deeper divides between your authentic self and other people. You become irrational and are prone to outbursts of truly detestable behaviors toward other people. You may have lost control of your inner narrative and allowed your fears to pour out through biased, bigoted, and deeply destructive remarks.

Instincts

Self-Preservation Six

If you are a Self-Preservation Six, you are more focused on building security and stability through mutual responsibility and reciprocal partnerships. You focus your energy on cultivating a safe space for you to be able to manage or play out your anxiety and fear. You do not hide your fears from others and oftentimes will use your insecurity as a way of gaining support and guidance. You tend to make friends slowly and maintain boundaries until you are completely certain you can trust the other person and are sure they will have your back, much like the energy of an Eight. Oftentimes you will experience disconnects with others when you feel your resources are being threatened, similar to Five energy. You rely on creating dependencies and making sure you have backup plans for when things will inevitably go wrong, even when everything is going right. The Self-Preservation instinct in Six makes you an individual who has made peace with the fact that anxiety and worry control your life, but you also can experience moments of true courage when you step out of the anxiety and allow yourself to trust other people and yourself. The Self-Preservation instinct in Six can create some challenges when connecting with others but also enables you to be a loyal person who will ride out the storm with a friend, much like Two energy. As a Self-Preservation Six you become the ride-or-die friend that people count on when everyone else has abandoned them.

Social Six

As a Social Six you tend to be slightly more extroverted than the other Instincts in Six, as you enjoy making connections and sharing your warmth and generosity with others, much like the energy of a healthy Two. You are more socially motivated than the other Instincts in Six, but also need space to process your fears around security and support. You can have a hard time working on developing your own identity or growing as an individual, much like the Nine energy. Instead of finding what works for you personally you tend to rely on group consensus and allow others to influence your beliefs and behaviors. When healthy, you are deeply loyal and will hold a group together, much like Eight energy, and you enjoy becoming part of something bigger than yourself. You can revert to passive-aggressive behaviors like Nines when you become frustrated or let your anxiety take over. This can present a challenge when you drop into unhealthy Levels of Development and become pessimistic and spiteful. However, when you move beyond fear and into a trusting space, you can establish long-lasting bonds with many different types of people and become the person who will make major sacrifices to protect your group and keep everyone safe and secure.

Sexual Six

If you identify as a Sexual Six, you may focus your energy on finding ways to either make yourself appear strong and in control like Eights; or like Fours who can actively seek out a rescuer, you will find people you can bond with who will provide security and support. You can use this outward display of strength, power, and control either personally or by proxy, to calm your fears and anxiety around being left without guidance or support. Much like Eight energy, you tend to test others in the hope of confirming your own security and stability. This can lead to some challenges with trying to maintain relationships when the other person is always being questioned or challenged. As a Sexual Six you carry the most doubt and distrust both of yourself and others, as you are constantly trying to calm your anxiety by challenging your situations and the people you care about. When healthy, you can add a deeper level of intimacy to any relationship as long as you find the ability to establish self-confidence and move into a space of open communication and trust.

Challenges and Overcoming the Egoic Agenda

As a Six you may harbor a deep distrust in all things: self, people, information, systems, and authority, among others. This can lead to serious complications when you try to maintain your relationships while allowing your fear to control you. The deep fear of losing guidance, support, and stability may cause you to become trapped in your head, paralyzed by fear and anxiety. On the surface you may appear to be a prepared and considerate human; however, your fear at Point Six is equally as powerful as your courage.

Playing out scenarios and weighing the benefits and risks associated with whatever decision needs to be made, whether big or small, is a way of navigating daily life, but it can also become an incapacitating pattern. The need for security in all things stems from the fear and anxiety associated with the self-doubt around the ability to function without guidance. You often find it difficult to trust; this is true in regard to trusting other people, but it also applies to trusting yourself. There is no need to allow your fear to paralyze you in your search for guidance. It is a counterproductive way of moving through the world and can be uninviting and disheartening to people around you, which can amplify disconnects across relationships and leave you with even more uncertainty than before.

You already have everything that
you need to chart your course.

If you must, do it afraid and let the
energy of trust propel you forward.

The Path of Inner Work

The Six's personal challenge, or passion of fear, as it is called in the Enneagram, is a deep distrust of all things: self, people, information, authority, actions, beliefs, behaviors. Your Six energy seeks out anything that may render you vulnerable, unstable, or without guidance and support. You look for the worst-case scenario and see all possible outcomes, positive and negative, but you are mainly focused on the negative. The intensity that your Six energy brings to everything matters and drives you to fall into a cynical and pessimistic space, which only fuels your fear and anxiety. This conscripted stance is the default to redirect your fears and attempt to remain in your comfort zone, refusing to be open to new ideas and perspectives or to trust anyone who challenges your comfort zone. Your unique way of navigating challenges can lead you to a paralyzing pattern of panic, distrust, and helplessness, a concept that is taught as the fixation of cowardice. This is where you get trapped and your fear becomes the guidance for your automatic pilot. The outbursts of paranoia and fear to project your anxiety onto others is your way of masking your Achilles' heel: trust. The invitation to move into a healthy space is attainable when you access the gift of inner strength and trust in yourself at Point Three, moving away from fear, anxiety, and cowardice as they are virulent emotions that are blocking your true heart. Enter the transformative space of the Body Center at Point Nine, where you can reclaim your focus and courage, taught in the Enneagram as the Six's virtue. This is where you will find your balance and confidence and release the incessant grip your fear has had on your life.

Responses to Conflicts

Unhealthy Reaction

Distrust; avoidance; external blame; irrational defensiveness; cowardice; inflexibility; passive-aggressive behavior; ambivalence; highly reactive and defensive; dividing others into group; irrational outbursts of panicked paranoia; radical response to "outsiders;" fanaticism; violent outbursts in extreme cases; adamantly defending your way of thinking in order to dismiss or demean anything that may challenge your stability; making insensitive comments; lacking in empathy and genuine emotion

Healthy Reaction

Truth-seeking; challenging of status quo or destructive leadership; willing to make sacrifices; courageous; speaking out against threats to collective security and safety; standing up and finding solutions when witnessing unfair practices harming other people; remaining loyal to your beliefs when acting from a kindhearted and courageous space; recognizing your fear as a wake-up call to take action you are no longer paralyzed by your anxiety; you stand up and fight against any challenge to the stability and security of any human or group, cutting through the false narratives and the negativity with courage and compassion

Finding Your Place at Point Six

We asked individuals to describe their Enneagram journey to help illustrate how the energy is expressed at each of the Enneagram points. Point Six is represented by Christy's journey.

I first took a free "test" to narrow in on a few types. I then read about each type in The Wisdom of the Enneagram. *The "test" results pointed me toward a type that I could not relate to, so I then took the RHETI, which felt like support for my results and focused more specifically on my type. I still had many questions and wanted to find out more before I could be sure about where I stood on the Enneagram map.*

When I read about my type in The Wisdom of the Enneagram, *I felt like someone had opened my head and read my thoughts. I felt exposed and understood in the most vulnerable of ways. It felt scary and uncertain to be so seen—as if I was naked and no longer able to hide, avoid, or deny.*

Initially, the journey felt harsh and rugged. I felt as if I was working in the resistance to change all of the patterns. And then a second phase of the journey came about where I could compassionately turn toward the patterns and see the brilliance and beauty of them and hold the limitations of them. The journey since then has been unfolding, revealing, and opening to more of self, others, and all that is.

I trust the journey and know that I am on a path cosmically set. I'm learning to actively participate and engage. I'm more able to taste the sweetness and savory, delighting in both. The vessel feels ever-expanding and contained to hold all that is here in joy and sorrow. And I keep stepping, stepping, and stepping...

CHRISTY, UNITED STATES

REFLECTIONS FOR POINT SIX

❖ How do you resonate with the basic fear at Point Six?

❖ How does the basic desire at Point Six manifest for you?

❖ How do you resonate with the core wound at Point Six?

❖ Consider the energy at Point Six: What do you feel is missing from your being?

❖ What are you searching for?

❖ What does it look like when you feel anxious, unprepared, or uncertain about the future?

Point Seven: *The Enthusiast*

Spontaneous, Versatile, Acquisitive, Scattered

"I am good or okay if I am happy and I am getting what I need."

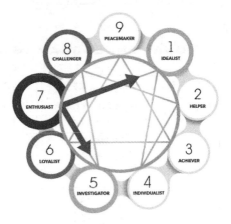

Basic Desire: To be happy, satisfied, and content, to have the freedom of choice, to have needs fulfilled

Basic Fear: To be deprived, to be in pain or experience suffering, to feel trapped, to have freedom compromised

Core Motivation: To maintain own freedom and happiness, to avoid missing out on worthwhile experiences, to stay excited and occupied, to avoid and deny pain and trauma

Core Wound: Self-indulgence—disconnection from nurturing figure: *"I must keep myself busy, amused, and entertained to block out the anxiety and fear."*

TRADITIONAL ENNEAGRAM LANGUAGE

PASSION	FIXATION	VIRTUE
GLUTTONY	PLANNING	SOBRIETY

⬇ ⬇ ⬇

TRANSITIONAL ENNEAGRAM LANGUAGE

Manifestation of Suffering in Our Shadow Side	Pattern of Behavior When Trapped by Personal Challenge	Releasing Ego Agenda & Stepping into Essence of Being
a deep desire to take on more of whatever life has to offer in order to avoid conflict, pain, or feeling trapped	*a paralyzing pattern of constantly looking for the next best thing, always moving forward, never looking back in search of whatever may bring happiness*	*a presence and stillness grounded in authentic internal reflection while accepting the reality of what is and not what could be*

Examples of Seven Energy: The Dalai Lama, James Baldwin, John F. Kennedy, Eddie Murphy, Elton John, Robin Williams, Jim Carrey, Ram Dass, Leonardo DiCaprio, Howard Stern, Jeff Bezos, Joe Biden, Sarah Palin, George W. Bush, Betty White, Edward VIII, Duke of Windsor, Thomas Jefferson, Benjamin Franklin, Amelia Earhart, Malcolm Forbes, Richard Branson, Ted Turner, Suze Orman

Wings

Seven has wing access to Point Eight and Point Six

SEVEN WITH AN EIGHT WING

AUTHENTIC SELF	SHADOW SELF
self-confident and assertive	impatient and blunt
calm during difficult situations	cold and harsh
positive and uplifting for others	self-centered and scattered when dealing with others
naturally charismatic	

SEVEN WITH A SIX WING

AUTHENTIC SELF	SHADOW SELF
sensitive to others' feelings	anxiety and self-doubt
optimistic in difficult situations	easily bored
productive	scattered focus
cooperative	disconnected from emotional honesty

"Too much self-centered attitude brings isolation. Result: loneliness, fear, anger. The extreme self-centered attitude is the source of suffering."

DALAI LAMA

Lines & Arrows

Seven has lines with arrows that connect to Point One and Point Five

SEVEN TO ONE

AUTHENTIC SELF	*SHADOW SELF*
more focused on others	self-centered
aware of the impact of actions and behaviors	deeply judgmental
principled	overly confident
grounded	dismissive of others and own feelings

SEVEN TO FIVE

AUTHENTIC SELF	*SHADOW SELF*
find calming stillness in self-reflection	avoid accountability
thoughtful and kind	self-centered
satiated	detached from others
focused	narcissistic beliefs

"When you are kind to someone in trouble, you hope they'll remember and be kind to someone else. And it'll become like a wildfire."

WHOOPI GOLDBERG

Summary

Thích Nhất Hạnh, a Vietnamese Thiền Buddhist monk, taught us many things throughout his 95 years on this planet. He once said, "We have the tendency to run away from suffering and to look for happiness. But, in fact, if you have not suffered, you have no chance to experience real happiness." If you stand at Point Seven, these words may hit you differently than other Enneagram energies. As a Seven you strive for happiness, as we all do, but your pursuit of satisfaction and contentment is a lifelong quest designed to keep you from dipping back down into the pain you have experienced. You are undoubtedly an outgoing and joyful person who thrives on adventure and excitement; you enjoy sampling all things life has to offer. There is an unmistakable energy that resides within you, and it can be felt by everyone you come in contact with throughout your life. This energy is designed to keep you perpetually moving forward, rarely looking back, and constantly searching for new experiences, new adventures, new knowledge, new anything. Beneath all of this movement and energy is usually a deeply repressed sense of dread and pain that you will get trapped if you stop or allow yourself to acknowledge what's underneath your buoyancy and joy. There are different reasons behind the perpetual motion and active resistance against anything that may feel like you are being trapped or deprived of your freedom. For the Seven, this perpetual energy can usually be traced back to ,a deep fear of being forced to deal with real emotions or an uncomfortable internal narrative.

If the dominant energy you experience is at Point Seven, you may feel compelled by a need to seek out fulfillment and satisfaction in whatever form that may take for you personally. You often experience a forward motion that keeps you from falling too deeply into any uncomfortable emotional state. Optimism, curiosity, versatility, freedom, and a general appreciation for seeking out experiences create the comfort zone for you. Many people who stand at Point Seven navigate life by avoiding pain and suffering, oftentimes feeling the need to redirect their attention as a way of maintaining their freedom of choice. The experience of being seen as a person who lacks compassion, sensitivity, or consideration may be a recurring theme for you at Point Seven. Your aversion to suffering may lead you to sidestep true compassion and empathy, a maneuver that many find cold and heartless. This is a disconnect that can be addressed and reestablished through presence and stillness. Even if your actions are well-intentioned, you may be unaware of the true impact of your words and behaviors when you try to remove yourself from discomfort or conflict.

Levels of Development

Healthy

As a healthy Seven you can establish your presence with principled focus and resilience, leading with awareness and profound vision in the face of divisiveness, confrontation, and conflict. You have found stillness and sobriety in the ability to access your authentic self and take right action with laser focus rather than a scattered approach to avoiding pain. The need to find outlets for deflecting pain in the hope of maintaining a false sense of freedom is transformed into a warning system for you to wake up, slow down, and become present. You no longer bounce from experience to experience, and you are able to acknowledge and find joy in the moment without having to always seek out something new or better. The extraordinary ability to find true happiness and create connections across differences with Grace and optimism is truly astonishing when you step into your true self.

Average

Most humans reside within these average levels and fluctuate up or down depending on the circumstances they find themselves in. As you drop down into the average Levels of Development, the ego agenda begins to take over. The fluctuations can create opportunities for you to pause and cultivate the presence needed to examine your thoughts and actions and course correct.

This allows you to move up in the levels and avoid falling back into unhealthy patterns of behavior and thought. However, as the ability for honest self-reflection and course correction wanes, you can become scattered and tactless, reticent to engage authentically in real emotional honesty for more than a fleeting moment. When challenges arise you can see opportunities to assert yourself and use your natural-born talents, but as you drop into the levels, you choose to stay disengaged and dismissive. You can become emotionally stunted; in deflecting your authentic self you are now self-seeking and uncomfortable with engaging or remaining present in any space that has conflict or negativity. The anxiety of feeling trapped can cause you to drop further in the levels instead of allowing your authentic self to shine. You can become passive at the sheer volume of suffering in the world and feel a cold detachment to other people's feelings and what is happening all around you.

You may find a short-lived presence and experience a calming sensation when you are able to channel healthy habits. You are able to find a clear focus on how to engage in life, but the fear of getting trapped and not being able to escape the monotony or the fear of jeopardizing your freedom quickly shifts you back into your deflection and evasion tactics. The fear and anxiety at these levels can morph into a combination of deflection, avoidance, and self-centered behaviors and cause you to drop further down the levels. You can use these moments of reflection as a wake-up call to step into a healthy space or allow them to deteriorate into a toxic pattern of thoughts and behaviors. It takes a great deal of self-reflection and inner work to rise through the levels and avoid dropping further.

Unhealthy

As you drop into the unhealthy levels, you become extremely narcissistic, unstable, insensitive, cynical, vindictive, and delusional. You begin to justify your actions and beliefs from the unhealthy energy of Point Seven. You often inadvertently become trapped in your self-inflicted unhappiness and pain, and feeling helpless you react impulsively and erratically to avoid any real emotional honesty. Fear, denial, and the repression of unhealed wounds are the primary motivators that distort your reality, resulting in a disdain for anything that feels like a challenge to your happiness or freedom. This disconnect may trigger your deep fear of becoming present to yourself, leading to an irresponsible pattern of acting out in panic and heedlessness. As you drop lower into the unhealthy levels, you are only covering up and defending against unhealed wounds that you refuse to truly acknowledge.

Instincts

Self-Preservation Seven

As a Self-Preservation Seven, you tend to be highly ambitious and work hard to make sure you maintain enough freedom—financial, professional, or personal— to be able to fulfill your own needs and do as you please. You may focus your energy on cultivating a life where you can maximize your experiences and fulfill your desires without having to rely too heavily on anyone or anything, similar to the energy of a Five or an Eight. You can be socially motivated, as Sevens tend to be more extroverted than not, but you unknowingly hold on to a deep anxiety around becoming too attached to anyone for fear of feeling trapped or bogged down. Oftentimes as a Self-Preservation Seven, you can emulate One energy when you become frustrated or unhappy, as you become critical, demanding, and judgmental of others. When you dip down into the unhealthy levels, the repressed fear and pain you have ignored bubble up and can cause you to be thoughtless and highly insensitive when communicating with people who threaten your way of life. The Self-Preservation instinct in Seven can create some challenges when connecting with others, but when healthy it can also foster an energy that is inviting, warm, and full of joy, which makes for a delightful companion who is down for any adventure.

Social Seven

If you are a Social Seven, you have probably spent considerable time cultivating a group of friends who share similar interests and are ready to take on any adventure. You tend to extend your energy outward by getting involved in social causes, groups, or community activities, much like the crusading energy of a One. While you enjoy getting involved, your natural tendency to allow your fear of feeling trapped or deprived of freedom makes you feel anxious as you get too comfortable or too ingrained into a single activity or group. This can cause an internal conflict between your commitment to stick with a cause or group and your desire to feel free and able to choose your own path. When healthy, you can be deeply impactful and bring a sense of joy and inspirational energy to any group and you enjoy becoming part of something bigger than yourself, much like the Six energy. You can easily withdraw and revert to evasive behaviors by abandoning people or groups when you feel overwhelmed by responsibility or obligation, much like the energy of an unhealthy Five. This can present a challenge when you drop into unhealthy Levels of Development and become narcissistic and callous with other people's emotions. However, when you move beyond the fear of feeling deprived or trapped you can establish long-lasting bonds with many different types of people and become the person who brings joy, friendliness, charm, and warmth to any group or situation.

Sexual Seven

If you identify as a Sexual Seven, you may focus your energy on finding new experiences and adventures in everything you do—much like the energy of a Four you seek out uniqueness and reject the ordinary. You thrive on feeling alive and taking in all that life has to offer, and can often bring this energy to your friends and social groups. You do not have a hard time connecting with people, as you are probably comfortable being outspoken, extroverted, and not afraid to strike up a conversation with anyone. In all likelihood you have never met a stranger; you have the natural ability to connect to anyone and bring people together from all walks of life. The downside to this energy is the predisposition to get bored easily and to allow your perpetual forward movement to prevent you from sticking with any one person, group, or situation for too long. Much like Four energy, you tend to romanticize relationships, enjoying the beginning stages of getting to know someone and the excitement that comes with the unknown. But like unhealthy Sexual Ones, you can become hardened by the reality of what is and move on to what could be. This can lead to some challenges with trying to maintain connections when you leave a wake of unfulfilled commitments and jilted relationships as you bounce to something new. When healthy, you have the ability to add a deeper level of curiosity and appreciation for diversity in all things—people, experiences, cultures, hobbies, traditions, and so on—to any group or relationship. As a Sexual Seven, it is important to commit to working on your ability to stay present long enough to enjoy all the wonderful things you have access to in your life right now.

Challenges and Overcoming the Egoic Agenda

When you begin to look inward and deal with your real pain and trauma, there can be a deeply wounded and repressed human sometimes hidden under a buoyant exterior. Despite your constant momentum and planning for future experiences, you may still be able to find joy in or bring joy to almost anything you do. But are you willing to consider the price of your happiness in regard to what it costs you in your relationships?

The deep fear of being deprived of your freedom, or trapped in pain and suffering may cause you to avoid dealing with conflict, situations, or people who challenge your freedom of choice. You may have a deep desire to try to stay positive and take in all that life has to offer by overindulging and bouncing from experience to experience, never actually becoming present to the reality of what you are experiencing. This progressive outlook on life can be a double-edged sword: an enterprising vision or an avoidance tactic. If this resonates with you, remember this: your search for happiness and contentment will be a hollow victory if you never become still enough to acknowledge what you have buried deep down and are now trying to conceal. It is a counterproductive way of moving through the world that can lead you to develop a strong aversion to anything even remotely uncomfortable, which robs you of real opportunities to find happiness through growth.

You have more ideas before breakfast than most people have in a lifetime.

Only some of them are good ideas. Slow your roll.

The Path of Inner Work

The Seven's personal challenge, or passion of gluttony as it is called in the Enneagram, is a deep desire to take on life and experience anything and everything it has to offer. Your Seven energy seeks more experiences, more fun, more distractions, more of everything. The intensity that your Seven energy brings into everything matters and drives you to push the limits in your life, never actually committing to one thing at a time or letting yourself experience something fully. This conscripted stance is the default to never let anything trap you or take away your freedom of choice. Your unique way of navigating challenges can lead you to deflection of the authentic self and a redirection of focus on anything that allows you to feel satisfied, a concept that is taught as the fixation of planning. This is where you get trapped and your deeply repressed fear becomes the guidance for your automatic pilot. The hyperactivity, perpetual motion forward, and the refusal to remain present or still for too long is your way of masking your Achilles' heel: addressing your unacknowledged internal trauma and your coping mechanisms. The invitation to move into a healthy space is attainable when you access the gift of grounded energy at Point One, moving away from fear, gluttony, and planning as they are distractions that are blocking access to your true heart and authentic self. Enter the transformative space at Point Five, where you can reclaim your sobriety, taught in the Enneagram as the Seven's virtue. This is where you will find your balance and focus to reclaim true happiness and connection.

Responses to Conflicts

Unhealthy Reaction

Avoidance; using inappropriate humor; insensitivity; cutting people out of your life; complete denial; anger; overwhelmed exhaustion; feeling trapped, causing irrational outbursts; cynicism; "fight-or-flight";

self-centered stance; erratic mood swings; callous deflection of others' humanity; when triggered you can use your unhealthy energy to dismiss, demean, and dehumanize anyone or anything that forces you to brush up against the darkness lurking inside of you; may make jokes and point out the pain of others as a way to deflect the responsibility you have to access true compassion as a decent human being

Healthy Reaction

Pausing for presence; slowing down to honor emotions as they arise; using charisma to enable others; trailblazing visionary; positivity; inability to watch others suffering forces you into action to spread joy and happiness; general ability to stay positive during tough times and see the good in any situation; connecting people across differences using your innate ability to find the good in any situation; infectious positive energy and natural tenacity to bring vivacity and spontaneity to everything you do

Finding Your Place at Point Seven

We asked individuals to describe their Enneagram journey to help illustrate how the energy is expressed at each of the Enneagram points. Point Seven is represented by Milton's journey.

As a Seven I experience life with consistent peaks of stimulation. I used to think that when I was not stimulated I was bored, but in actuality, I was simply experiencing life at a normal level. I can easily range from overexcited to overanxious if I'm not grounded in my body. My brain moves at a rate of speed that used to make me think I had some form of ADHD. Thankfully I've learned to focus really well over the years. I'm usually able to flip anything to the positive if needed. When in the presence of others, I have a strong tendency to want to uplift them through humor or creative ideas.

At my best I am not too much Seven. I am able to use my unique thinking patterns to convey an optimistic vision with my brilliant ideas that inspire people into action. I bring joy and enthusiasm into the lives of others, giving them a boost of energy to go after their dreams. I'm also in touch with my heart, so I don't miss moments in the present nor do I avoid dealing with my own emotions.

At my worst, I am all over the place. I am scattered mentally. I am emotionally avoidant. I'm physically ripping and running because I've overbooked myself. I start moving faster than usual, and I am not able to keep up with my ego's addiction to being stimulated. Anxiety and anxiousness run pretty high because there's an avoidance of something deeper that is unresolved.

When I discovered I was a Seven, my first reaction was one of pride. My second reaction was one of feeling pinned down. I found out I was a Seven amongst a small group of church members with The Wisdom of the Enneagram *book by Riso and Hudson. The first two paragraphs were all the great things about being a Seven. The next two paragraphs were the opposite, so I was flabbergasted. Also, that being read out loud in a group really made me put my poker face on, but it intrigued me so much I had to learn more.*

When I've wandered off into the shadowland of unhealthy Seven, I find ways to ground myself and slow down. I have specific practices that I go to. Some include meditative walking, being still, conscious breathing, qigong, and centering prayer. Those practices help me in so many ways to come back to myself and be present in the moment.

MILTON, TENNESSEE

REFLECTIONS FOR POINT SEVEN

❖ How do you resonate with the basic fear at Point Seven?

❖ How does the basic desire at Point Seven manifest for you?

❖ How do you resonate with the core wound at Point Seven?

❖ Consider the energy at Point Seven: What are you searching for? Do you feel that something is missing from your being?

❖ What does it look like when you feel trapped or deprived of your freedom?

❖ How do you intentionally choose to avoid pain, and what does that look like for you?

Part III

FINDING YOUR PLACE ON THE ENNEAGRAM MAP

Chapter 6

Further Exploration into Deeper Components within the Enneagram

Don't be fooled by the title "Enneagram Made Easy." The Enneagram is, by nature, a complex and fluid system that encompasses a collective consciousness across various cultures and traditions over centuries. This book has only scratched the surface of what the Enneagram offers us. I encourage you to keep reading and exploring and dive deeper into the vastness of the Enneagram. Following are just a few components of the Enneagram that require further exploration as you progress along your journey.

Essence

At the core of our being we find our true self or "Essence." This is our soul connection to self from which we disconnected. In Christianity it is what was lost in the fall from Grace when man angered God and was cast out of the garden of Eden. In other spiritual traditions and cultures it is the separation from our Creator, the Universe, or Higher Power. Our life's journey is spent trying to repair and recapture that felt sense of wholeness—a wholeness that comes only when we uncover our authentic self, who is never separate from the Divine.

Core Wounds

The core wounds, sometimes referred to as the childhood wound, are nuanced and contain aspects of similarity and difference in individuals of the same type energy. Additionally, this is where nature versus nurture can come into play. The core wounds will also enter into the equation when we look at what is pushing you so hard in a particular direction. At every point, there is a core wound that plays an identifiable role in the formation of the personality structure. For example, the core wound for a person who stands at Point Three is based on the need for approval, which is satisfied by achievement and success. The egoic internalized childhood message is "I will be rejected and abandoned if I am not successful." While the circumstances may vary, the wounding is consistent and has a sustainable effect on the outcome of the energy of each of the nine points.

Shadow Work/Shadow Side

Any exploration into inner work will eventually lead you to come face to face with the shadow side of your being. The Enneagram is no different. The Swiss psychiatrist Carl Gustaf Jung introduced the concept of the shadow self. He used this term to describe the unconscious aspects of personality. Exploring these unconscious parts by engaging in inner work helps you to become aware of the health of your personality structure; and to strive to be as healthy in your personality construct as you would like to be in your physical body. When trying to determine your dominant Enneagram point/type it is important to look at the personality traits that represent your shadow self. Trying to find your dominant Enneagram point by connecting only to the upside of any point can lead to mistyping, confusion, and frustration.

Object Relations

Object relations are key to the development of the self/ego. The term *object* was originally introduced by Sigmund Freud. He used this term to describe any target or focus of instinctual impulses. Melanie Klein, who is often identified as the first object relations theorist, departed from Freud's viewpoint as she believed that a baby is born with drives that are relational in nature. There is an impressive lineage of psychologists and psychiatrists who have contributed to our evolving understanding of object relations work.

The inner work process of the Enneagram also takes us beyond things as objects. Our ego-self (invested belief in our personality structure) can only develop in relation to something/someone else. We delve into the observation of the human "objects" that we are in relationship with, and these instinctual drives are designed to help us adjust to and make sense of the human world.

Each Enneagram point/type has its own unique object relations orientation. The concept of object relations requires deep inner work and will take you further into your Enneagram journey.

The Three Components of Our Object Relations
Self/Ego—Other—Felt Sense

The Three Primary Others/Objects
Nurturing Figure—Protective Figure—Belonging Figure

The Three Intrinsic Affects
Attachment—Frustration—Rejection

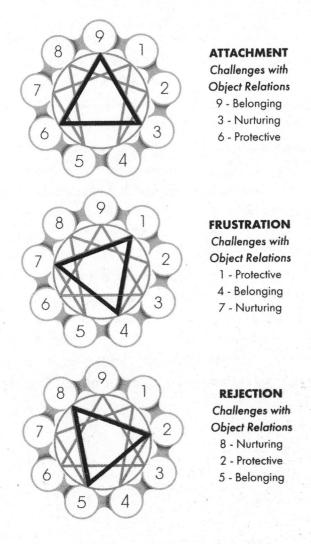

ATTACHMENT
Challenges with
Object Relations
9 - Belonging
3 - Nurturing
6 - Protective

FRUSTRATION
Challenges with
Object Relations
1 - Protective
4 - Belonging
7 - Nurturing

REJECTION
Challenges with
Object Relations
8 - Nurturing
2 - Protective
5 - Belonging

The Enneagram and object relations

Hornevian

The Enneagram Hornevian Groups are based on the Hornevian Model, named after Karen Horney, who first discovered that there were connections across the three Centers of Intelligence based on how people communicate and connect with others in order to get what they want. Karen Horney was a psychoanalyst who used Sigmund Freud's work to build upon the research of human nature in regard to social interaction and inner conflict resolution. While Horney did not connect the original Hornevian Model to the Enneagram, the early Enneagram teachers identified a clear connection in how this model fits in with how certain points could be grouped based on the stance taken during conflict or everyday communication. There are three Hornevian Groups: Compliant, Withdrawn, and Assertive. Enneagram Hornevian Groups show us how each Enneagram point interacts with other people in order to meet their own needs.

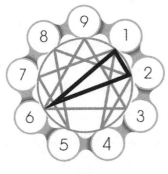

COMPLIANT
Move energy toward people
1 - earn autonomy
2 - earn attention
6 - earn security

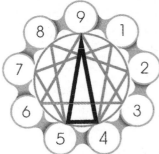

WITHDRAWN
Move energy away from people
9 - withdraw to gain autonomy
4 - withdraw to gain attention
5 - withdraw to gain security

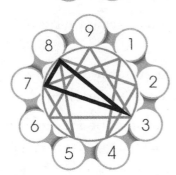

ASSERTIVE
Move energy against people
8 - demand autonomy
3 - demand attention
7- demand security

The Enneagram Hornevian groups

Compliant Group 1-2-6 (Cooperators)

The Compliant Group is focused on moving their energy inward and then toward people as a way of having their needs met. This group is concerned with their inner monologue to guide them to do what is "right" as it pertains to their Enneagram energy.

At Point One the energy is focused on following the rules to earn autonomy. At Point Two the energy is focused on helping others to earn attention. At Point Six the energy is focused on aligning with the group to earn stability and security.

Cooperators:

* Tend to be hardworking and committed

* Are willing to make sacrifices

* Show up and are dedicated to doing what is expected of them

* Can be more predictable and can get overwhelmed with spontaneous changes or uncertainty

* Have an awareness of how other people are involved in the situation and may feel the need to fall into support roles or positions of service to others

Withdrawn Group 9-4-5 (Soloists)

The Withdrawn Group is focused on moving their energy away from people as a way of having their needs met. This group tends to focus on retreating inward to allow themselves space to reflect and find their place within any given situation. The reasons behind the withdrawal and the way in which they move their energy away from people show up differently for each point.

At Point Nine the energy is focused away from conflict and distress to seek out peace. At Point Four the energy is focused inward to gain attention. At Point Five the energy is focused inward to the security of the inner sanctum.

Soloists:

- Tend to be more reserved, quiet, independent, and reflective
- Typically need more time to be introspective and receptive before they engage in a situation
- When they feel ready and prepared to respond, they can be very productive and efficient
- Oftentimes they can feel overwhelmed by large groups or "invasive" external influences
- Usually are uncomfortable taking the lead and making quick decisions without time to reflect

Assertive Group 8-3-7 (Initiators)

The Assertive Group moves their energy against people as a way of having their needs met. They focus their efforts on actively taking charge of a situation and demanding what they want, though this shows up differently for each point.

At Point Eight the energy is focused on moving against people to demand control and autonomy. At Point Three the energy is focused on moving against what gets in the way of seeking out attention and praise. At Point Seven the energy is focused on moving against whatever gets in the way of happiness, freedom, and security.

Initiators:

❖ Tend to be bold, extroverted, forceful, and independent

❖ Are willing to initiate projects and take charge of situations

❖ Tend to seize opportunities and strive to make things happen

❖ Usually know what they want and will actively go after whatever it may be

❖ Are inclined to be the leader, call the shots, and influence people

❖ Are prone to cutting through unnecessary details to get to the point of things

Harmonics

The Enneagram Harmonic Groups are triads that help us explore how each point or type manages conflict and challenges. Harmonic Groups also illustrate how we protect ourselves against disappointment or cope when we haven't had our needs met adequately. The three Enneagram Harmonic Groups are separated into the Positive Outlook Group, the Rational Competency Group, and the Emotional Realness Group. This particular aspect of the Enneagram structure is especially helpful when beginning your Enneagram journey and can facilitate your discovery of your dominant Enneagram energy. By looking at how you react to challenges in your life and comparing this reaction to the Harmonic Groups you can uncover a deeper connection to a particular Enneagram energy. Instead of focusing on multiple components within each type, the harmonics help to concentrate on how we function during the conflict. This way of looking at a particular Enneagram energy can help to combine the basic fear and desire and core motivation in a more manageable way. Looking at the triad groupings can also help you find your connection to other points within the same triad and may help you if you feel you have been mistyped.

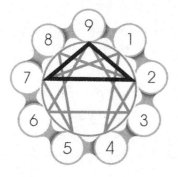

POSITIVE OUTLOOK

Redirect focus in a positive way

9 - focus on good in
environment & others

2 - focus on good in self

7 - focus on good experiences

RATIONAL COMPETENCY

Set aside emotion to focus on logic

1 - focus on doing the right thing

3 - focus on getting things done

5 - focus on problem solving

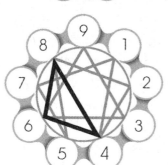

EMOTIONAL REALNESS

Use emotions to guide reactions

8 - outward expression to control

4 - embrace emotional responses

6 - outward expression of inner fear

The Enneagram Harmonic groups

Positive Outlook Group 9-2-7

The Positive Outlook Group consists of Points Nine, Two, and Seven. This group responds to conflict by redirecting focus to a positive outcome or reframing disappointment in a more positive manner. The Positive Outlook Group tends to have a hard time dealing with their own shadow side, which translates into the way they approach external conflicts. This group also has difficulty balancing their own needs with others.

Twos focus on others while actively ignoring their own needs. Sevens focus on their needs while neglecting the needs of others. Nines tend to fall short of fulfilling either in the process of trying to focus on both their needs and the needs of others.

Positive Outlook:

❖ Tends to smooth over problems

❖ Responds to conflict and difficulty by adopting a positive attitude

❖ Reframes disappointment

❖ Emphasizes the uplifting aspects of life and looks at the bright side

❖ Are morale builders who enjoy helping others feel good during a bad situation

Rational Competency Group 1-3-5

The Rational Competency Group is home to Point One, Three, and Five. This group focuses on setting aside emotions and personal needs and remaining objective, rational, and effective during conflict. The Rational Competency Group has a unique relationship with systems and structures and the way in which they navigate within these systems in order to get what they want.

Ones tend to follow rules and procedures because it is the right thing to do. Fives are prone to working outside of the confines of rules and systems, delving deep. Threes can have a healthy respect for systems but will enforce their freedom from restrictions.

Rational Competency:

❖ Tends to solve problems

❖ Puts aside their personal feelings

❖ Drives to be objective, competent, and effective

❖ Handles problems through analyzing, understanding, and deconstructing the situation to be able to fix it and move on

❖ Tends to remove emotions from the equation

Emotional Realness Group 8-4-6

The Emotional Realness Group, sometimes referred to as the Reactive Group, consists of Point Eight, Four, and Six. This group uses emotional responses to get what they need and tends to have strong opinions about what needs to be done. For the Emotional Realness Group, surfacing problems and expressing their feelings about those problems are usually front and center.

Eights tend to address problems head-on with a direct and strong emotional response that emphasizes their independence. Fours are prone to seeking out a complementary emotional response from others that supports their own emotions. Sixes tend to have a strong emotional response that serves as a defense against being affected by the problem.

Emotional Realness:

❖ Tends to surface problems

❖ Reacts to conflicts and problems with an emotional charge

❖ Can have difficulty trusting others

❖ Seeks out an emotional response from others that matches the level of intensity of their own emotional response

❖ Usually has strong likes and dislikes

Chapter 7

Finding Your Type/Point

If you are still searching for "home" on the Enneagram map, there are a few different avenues available to you. It is important to remember that no one can tell you your type, and you can take tests and quizzes and go through workshops to try to determine it. But if you take only one thing from this book, let it be this: this is a journey, not a destination. The Enneagram is vast and full of wisdom that would take many lifetimes to fully master. Below are a few helpful ways of finding your dominant Enneagram energy.

Panels

Over the years I have discovered that one of the most effective methods for helping people find their dominant Enneagram energy is through the experience of panels facilitated by a reputable Enneagram teacher. This process allows people to witness different perspectives from all nine types in real time. The experience gives participants the chance to actually *feel* the authentic energy of each point. Instead of reading through descriptors detailing the good, the bad, and the ugly of a personality structure, the participants are given an immersive experience. Panels are available online. I have participated in panels facilitated by Beatrice Chestnut, and I continue to encourage my students to access her videos online.

Tests, Quizzes, and Assessment Tools

In the past three decades I have watched thousands of people take Enneagram quizzes, tests, and assessments. There are some excellent assessment tools available; however, you will get the results of your input. Another way of saying this is: bad input, bad results. It is always interesting to see someone test as a certain Enneagram point when they are very clearly expressing strong characteristics present within another Enneagram point. It is difficult to be totally honest when taking these assessments. If the choices are "I am kind and generous" versus "I am mean and stingy," it's amazing how many people are always kind and generous. If you are going to invest money in an Enneagram test, you need to be as honest and authentic with your responses as humanly possible. If you do not feel like you are ready to strip down to your birthday suit, save your money. After you have done some exploration on your own you may be prepared to pick up the mirror and engage in authentic self-disclosure. We have a brief Enneagram quiz available on my website *(see page 257)*. Additionally, you will find online tests listed below that I am personally familiar with:

❖ RHETI

❖ QUEST

❖ IEQ9

❖ Riso-Hudson TAS

Defense Mechanisms

Recently I have found that using language people already understand to introduce them to a new concept is a very effective way to not only disseminate new information but to keep people engaged in the learning process. In my work teaching the Enneagram to therapists and psychologists, I have discovered that exploring the nine Enneagram types through looking at common defense mechanisms is quite efficient and can help people to identify their type in some cases.

Examples of Look-Alike Types

There are several look-alike types that appear to be similar based on surface-level behaviors. However, we must always remember that the Enneagram helps us to find our true place on the map based on our deeper motivations, not just surface-level behavior.

There are many different resources and books that focus solely on look-alike types and how to differentiate between similar energies. If you are beginning your Enneagram energy and find yourself wavering between two or more energies, we suggest seeking out these resources.

Remember to explore all types to understand the traits that many Enneagram energies share and keep an open mind when trying to differentiate between the points. Here are a few examples of some common look-alike types to help you understand how two different Enneagram energies can resemble each other.

Nine and Two

Nines and Twos resemble each other in that they are both generally helpful and willing to be of assistance when needed. However, there are a few differences between the Nine and the Two. First of all, Nines are usually not actively seeking out ways to help like the Two energy. When asked or presented with the opportunity to help, a healthy Nine is likely to offer a hand but might be second in line behind the Two. Additionally, Nine's aversion to conflict can place them on the back lines of a problematic situation, whereas the Two is charging head-on to deal with the tough stuff. Another clear distinction between the Nine and the Two is that the manipulative nature of the Two is front and center when they are operating in the average to unhealthy Levels of Development. The Nine energy does not have the same tendency to lean into manipulative behavior and oftentimes will cut clear through someone's facade and tell it like it is. In short, Twos lean in, Nines lean back.

Sevens and Threes

Sevens and Threes are similar in action and behavior, but when you dive deeper, the differences become quite apparent. Both are typically externally motivated, energetic, and strive to do great things. They aim for the top and are usually impressive, fun, vivacious people. Sevens enjoy the pursuit of things that make them happy and the stimulation of acquiring things like wealth, notoriety, or position because it is new and exciting. Threes also enjoy acquiring these things; however, they are typically more concerned with how other people view their success than with the actual experience. In regard to the process of moving through the world, Sevens are visionaries and Threes are achievers. Sevens are the creators of the ideas, but Threes are the people who make things happen. When faced with a seemingly no-win situation, Sevens will charge head-on or change course with little trepidation, whereas a Three will detach themselves from anything that looks like it is doomed to fail.

Mistyping

There is wisdom in learning why you have mistyped. You can spend your entire life focused on your type so much that you shift your perspective to mold yourself into what you think your type may be. A common experience we share as we begin our Enneagram journey is the temptation to avoid looking at our dominant point or type and instead to fit ourselves into the desirable aspects of other points across the Enneagram map. It is important to remember that not all of the characteristics and traits of the Enneagram energy you identify with may be present within your actions, beliefs, and behaviors. We are composed of all nine types/energies, leading with one dominant Enneagram energy, an instinct within that energy, influences from our wings and lines, and essential bits and pieces of each of the other Enneagram energies we pick up as we need them. A deeper inquiry into the Enneagram can provide us with ways of connecting why, how, and when different traits could appear.

Often, mistyping comes from people trying to see themselves the way they would like to be instead of how they really show up in the world.

Additionally, when taking tests or reading about types, many people will look at the way they are in the present and overlook the necessity of examining their behaviors before life begins to teach them lessons. For example, angry Eights in their teens and 20s learn that anger is not a welcomed guest in the workplace. They may lose several jobs before the recognition comes that life is trying to teach them to control their anger. This does not mean that the anger has gone away; it remains at the core, but the Eight learns to modify their behavior for survival. This is true for every type when we look at what is at the core of personality archetypes. To avoid mistyping, we must look at how we show up now and how we have shown up in the past.

A leisurely walk down memory lane allows you to surface situations, people, places, reactions, and responses. Facing the truth when we look in the mirror is sometimes difficult but necessary when we mistype. Remember, people are constantly giving feedback that might be useful when trying to find your point on the Enneagram map. Whatever you do, don't fall into the trap of believing that if you didn't get it right on the first go-round all is lost. I know more people who didn't nail it at first guess than people who did.

Read the books, study panels of the types online, attend live or virtual workshops whenever possible. Mistyping presents its own gifts as you get to experience shedding another version of yourself that you will no longer have to live up to. The real you is not too far away.

Conclusion

This book was designed to simplify and unpack the elements of the Enneagram that will be necessary for you in order to embark on your Enneagram journey. The hope is that you will go deeper into the Enneagram and recognize that the complexity that it contains will be life-changing. There are no shortcuts. The path that you are on has no definitive destination; this will be a lifelong journey. If you stay the course, the rewards that await you every step of the way will be well worth the time that you invest. Remember: the more you know about yourself, the better the quality of your relationships. Life is all about relationships.

I hope *Enneagram Made Easy* has jump-started your interest in learning more about the Enneagram. When I teach the Enneagram, people often say to me, "If only I had learned about this sooner." I believe this information will come to you at precisely the right time. Sooner may be good, but remember, now is better than never. It is never too late to recognize what is truly important to you. Your inner work with the Enneagram as your road map will lead you to discover things about yourself that you never knew and help you understand the why underneath it all.

If you take the time to learn about how you show up in the world, the reward that you will receive is beyond measure. There will always be some who feed into the chaos and confusion in the world. Your engagement with the people you encounter on your journey will either contribute to the disorder or create a safe space for yourself and others. I believe that people who are willing to be present with one another can cultivate safe space and trust. This is not about agreeing with everyone's thoughts, views, or actions. It is coming together to create internal space as individuals who understand and respect each other. Creating this internal spaciousness leaves room for something new to arise. Understanding leads to respect and opens a passageway for love and acceptance. When we pause and reflect we can see how we have flawed expectations. We seek to have authentic connections and want to appreciate the experience of deep love without understanding the self first. You cannot give to another something that you don't have.

Self-love, cultivated with understanding and appreciation for our unique gifts and unlimited potential, allows for the evolution of enlightenment. The word *enlightenment* is derived from Latin and Greek, with *en* meaning into, and *light* has its roots in Old English, meaning the concept of photons that illuminate, brighten, or clarify. Many people seek enlightenment with no idea of what it means. In the simplest words possible it means to bring clarity to knowledge. We are here at this present moment with unprecedented access to information. Information when integrated becomes knowledge. When given the choice between having clarity about whatever knowledge that you have gained in your lifetime or willful ignorance, seek the high road. Becoming present with yourself by allowing your inner witness to observe the way you move through each day will give you insight into your own being. We can improve our interactions by breathing before speaking, and pausing long enough to intentionally choose our words. When we make the choice to heal ourselves we will also begin the work of healing all of humanity. I hope for humanity's sake that you make yourself a priority in your life and learn to love yourself.

Let the Enneagram teach you how to love yourself. Your life and the lives of everyone around you will be forever changed.

Caritas.

Deborah Egerton

Resources

Further information can be found at:
DeborahEgerton.com/resources

Quiz: DeborahEgerton.com/enneagram

Further Reading

You may also like to read my other books:

Know Justice Know Peace: A Transformative Journey of Social Justice, Anti-Racism, and Healing through the Power of the Enneagram (2022)

The Enneagram Inner Work Journal Series

The Enneagram Type 1 Journal: Inner Work for the Idealist

The Enneagram Type 2 Journal: Inner Work for the Helper

The Enneagram Type 3 Journal: Inner Work for the Achiever

The Enneagram Type 4 Journal: Inner Work for the Individualist

The Enneagram Type 5 Journal: Inner Work for the Investigator

The Enneagram Type 6 Journal: Inner Work for the Loyalist

The Enneagram Type 7 Journal: Inner Work for the Enthusiast

The Enneagram Type 8 Journal: Inner Work for the Challenger

The Enneagram Type 9 Journal: Inner Work for the Peacemaker

Acknowledgments

I began working on this project during a month-long journey through Egypt. During the trip, my three Centers of Intelligence went into overdrive. My mind was overstimulated, my heart was wide open, and my body was challenged by the rigorous terrain we covered. My companions on this trip came from different parts of the world to deepen our understanding of the Enneagram—another group of seekers. I want to express my deep gratitude to these incredible individuals whose contributions made the creation of *Enneagram Made Easy* possible. Your support, wisdom, and heartfelt stories of your experiences with the Enneagram have profoundly enriched this book.

First and foremost, I would like to thank Lisi Mohandessi, my cowriter, Creative Director, and cherished friend. We have often laughed when we come up with the same idea simultaneously. I cannot say enough about our families' unwavering encouragement and understanding throughout this writing journey. Your love and belief fueled my determination to see this project through.

I extend my heartfelt appreciation to my mentors and advisors, whose guidance and expertise opened new doors of knowledge and understanding in the realm of the Enneagram. Your wisdom and insights have significantly shaped the content of this book.

A special mention goes to the Enneagram experts and practitioners who generously shared their vast wealth of knowledge and experiences with me. Your expertise and passion for the Enneagram have inspired me to delve deeper into its intricacies, allowing me to present a comprehensive and accessible guide for all readers.

I extend my gratitude to the editors at Hay House, who provided valuable feedback and constructive criticism during the editing process. Your attention to detail and keen insights have greatly improved the clarity and impact of this book.

Lastly, but certainly not least, I want to express my profound thanks to the readers and enthusiasts of the Enneagram who have supported and championed my work. Your enthusiasm and engagement have motivated me to continue exploring this fascinating field and sharing its transformative power with the world.

You have all played an invaluable role in bringing *Enneagram Made Easy* to life. Your contributions have made this book an actual labor of love, and I am forever grateful for your presence in my life.

Caritas,

Deborah Egerton

Deborah Threadgill Egerton, Ph.D.

About the Author

Deborah Threadgill Egerton, Ph.D., is an internationally respected psychotherapist, spiritual teacher, best-selling author, Certified Enneagram teacher, IEA Accredited Professional with Distinction, and President of the International Enneagram Association. She has dedicated her life to sharing the Enneagram as a powerful mechanism for healing designed to rekindle a gentler, more compassionate approach to inner work. Her profound passion lies in guiding others to discover the depths of their own humanity, while fostering a heartfelt recognition and reverence for the humanity that unites us all. With unwavering dedication, she aspires to cultivate a world brimming with love and kindness. She encourages us all to partake in the transformative journey of inner healing through the enriching practice of the Enneagram's profound self-discovery.

For more information on Dr. Egerton's work please visit:

DeborahEgerton.com

TrinityTransition.com

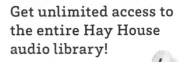